Table of Contents

I

P9-APO-933

Directions: Match the numbers 1–20. The first one is done for you.

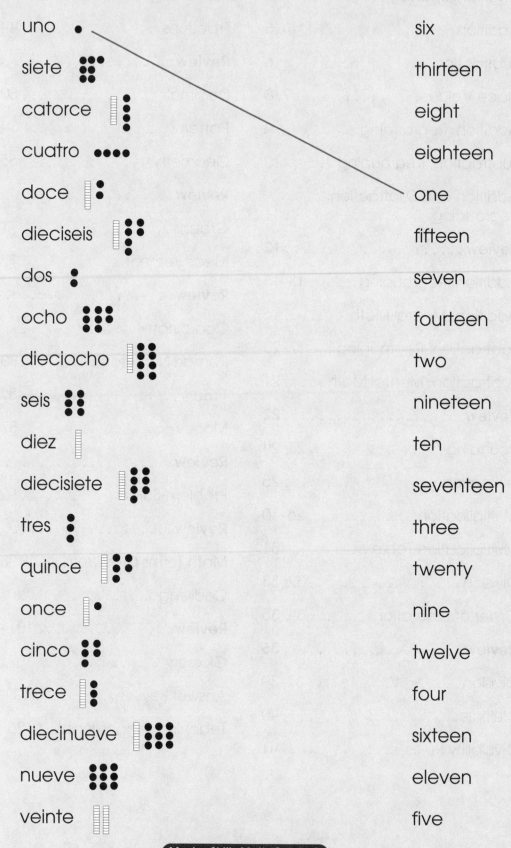

uno •   six

siete   thirteen

catorce   eight

cuatro ••••   eighteen

doce   one

dieciseis   fifteen

dos •   seven

ocho   fourteen

dieciocho   two

seis   nineteen

diez   ten

diecisiete   seventeen

tres   three

quince   twenty

once   nine

cinco   twelve

trece   four

diecinueve   sixteen

nueve   eleven

veinte   five

Addition means *"putting together"* or adding two or more numbers to find the sum. For example, 3 + 5 = 8.

"Más" means *plus* in Spanish.

Example: uno   más   tres = ___4___

    1   +   3

Directions: Add to find the answer.

siete más catorce = _____   nueve más veinte = _____

cuatro más doce = _____   once más quince = _____

dieciseis más dos = _____   ocho más uno = _____

cinco más tres = _____   diez más seis = _____

tres más diez = _____

Addition

Example:

Add the ones.

$$\begin{array}{r} 26 \\ + 21 \\ \hline 7 \end{array}$$

Add the tens.

$$\begin{array}{r} 26 \\ + 21 \\ \hline 47 \end{array}$$

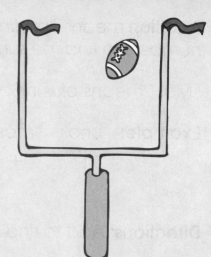

Directions: Add.

$$\begin{array}{r} 18 \\ + 11 \\ \hline \end{array} \qquad \begin{array}{r} 24 \\ + 35 \\ \hline \end{array} \qquad \begin{array}{r} 38 \\ + 21 \\ \hline \end{array} \qquad \begin{array}{r} 49 \\ + 50 \\ \hline \end{array}$$

$$\begin{array}{r} 75 \\ + 12 \\ \hline \end{array} \qquad \begin{array}{r} 83 \\ + 16 \\ \hline \end{array} \qquad \begin{array}{r} 67 \\ + 32 \\ \hline \end{array} \qquad \begin{array}{r} 44 \\ + 25 \\ \hline \end{array}$$

$68 + 20 = \underline{\hspace{1cm}}$ $\qquad\qquad$ $54 + 25 = \underline{\hspace{1cm}}$

The Lions scored 42 points. The Clippers scored 21 points. How many points were scored in all? $\underline{\hspace{2cm}}$

Directions: Follow the plays of your favorite team.

A touchdown is worth 6 points.
A field goal is worth 3 points.

GO _____
WRITE YOUR TEAM HERE!

 2 touchdowns = _____ points

 I touchdown + 2 field goals = _____ points

 3 field goals = _____ points

 I field goal + I touchdown = _____ points

Your team won the game and made record-breaking points! How many points did they score in all? _____

Subtraction

Subtraction means *"taking away"* or subtracting one number from another to find the difference. For example, $10 - 3 = 7$.

Example: Subtract the ones.   Subtract the tens.

$$\begin{array}{r} 39 \\ -\,24 \\ \hline 5 \end{array} \qquad\qquad \begin{array}{r} 39 \\ -\,24 \\ \hline |5 \end{array}$$

Directions: Subtract.

$$\begin{array}{r} 48 \\ -\,35 \\ \hline \end{array} \qquad \begin{array}{r} 95 \\ -\,22 \\ \hline \end{array} \qquad \begin{array}{r} 87 \\ -\,16 \\ \hline \end{array} \qquad \begin{array}{r} 55 \\ -\,43 \\ \hline \end{array}$$

$$\begin{array}{r} 37 \\ -\,14 \\ \hline \end{array} \qquad \begin{array}{r} 69 \\ -\,57 \\ \hline \end{array} \qquad \begin{array}{r} 44 \\ -\,23 \\ \hline \end{array} \qquad \begin{array}{r} 99 \\ -\,78 \\ \hline \end{array}$$

$66 - 44 =$ _____ $57 - 33 =$ _____

The yellow car traveled 87 miles per hour. The orange car traveled 66 miles per hour. How much faster was the yellow car traveling?

_____

Place Value

The place value of a digit, or numeral, is shown by where it is in the number. For example, in the number 1,234, 1 has the place value of thousands, 2 is hundreds, 3 is tens, and 4 is ones.

Hundred Thousands	Ten Thousands	Thousands	Hundreds	Tens	Ones
9	4	3	8	5	2

Directions: Match the numbers in Column A with the words in Column B. The first one is done for you.

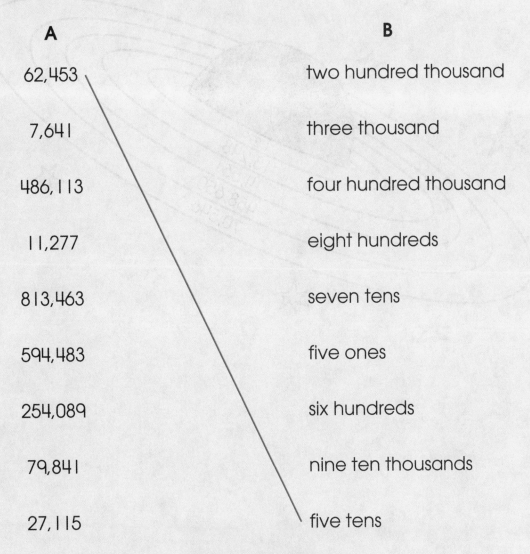

A	B
62,453	two hundred thousand
7,641	three thousand
486,113	four hundred thousand
11,277	eight hundreds
813,463	seven tens
594,483	five ones
254,089	six hundreds
79,841	nine ten thousands
27,115	five tens

Directions: Use the code to color the rings.

If the number has:
seven ten thousands, color it **red**.
one thousand, color it **blue**.
four hundred thousands, color it **green**.
six tens, color it **brown**.
eight ones, color it yellow.

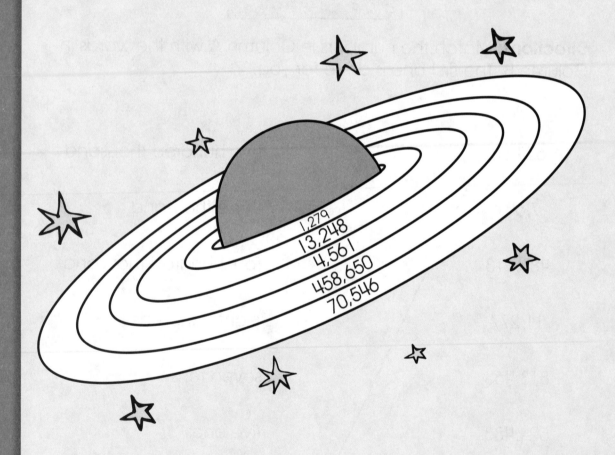

1,279
13,248
4,561
458,650
70,546

Addition: Regrouping

Addition means "putting together" or adding two or more numbers to find the sum. To regroup is to use 10 ones to form one ten, 10 tens to form one hundred, and so on.

Example:

Add the ones.

```
  88
+ 21
   9
```

Add the tens with regrouping.

```
  88
+ 21
 109
```

Directions: Add using regrouping.

```
  37        56        51        37
+ 72      + 67      + 88      + 55
```

```
  93        47        81        23
+ 54      + 82      + 77      + 92
```

92 + 13 = _____   73 + 83 = _____

The Blues scored 63 points. The Reds scored 44 points. How many points were scored in all? _____

Subtraction: Regrouping

Subtraction means "taking away" or subtracting one number from another to find the difference. To regroup is to use one ten to form 10 ones, one hundred to form 10 tens, and so on.

Example:

$$32 = 2 \text{ tens} + 12 \text{ ones}$$
$$- 13 = 1 \text{ ten} + 3 \text{ ones}$$
$$19 = 1 \text{ ten} + 9 \text{ ones}$$

Directions: Subtract using regrouping.

$$\begin{array}{r} 33 \\ -28 \\ \hline \end{array} \qquad \begin{array}{r} 86 \\ -59 \\ \hline \end{array} \qquad \begin{array}{r} 92 \\ -37 \\ \hline \end{array} \qquad \begin{array}{r} 71 \\ -48 \\ \hline \end{array}$$

$$\begin{array}{r} 63 \\ -47 \\ \hline \end{array} \qquad \begin{array}{r} 45 \\ -18 \\ \hline \end{array} \qquad \begin{array}{r} 31 \\ -22 \\ \hline \end{array} \qquad \begin{array}{r} 55 \\ -39 \\ \hline \end{array}$$

$$82 - 69 = \underline{\qquad} \qquad\qquad 73 - 36 = \underline{\qquad}$$

The Yankees won 85 games. The Cubs won 69 games. How many more games did the Yankees win?

_____

Directions: Add or subtract. Regroup when needed.

$$\begin{array}{r} 92 \\ -\ 47 \\ \hline \end{array} \qquad \begin{array}{r} 58 \\ +\ 26 \\ \hline \end{array} \qquad \begin{array}{r} 63 \\ +\ 18 \\ \hline \end{array} \qquad \begin{array}{r} 77 \\ -\ 38 \\ \hline \end{array}$$

$$\begin{array}{r} 27 \\ -\ 17 \\ \hline \end{array} \qquad \begin{array}{r} 31 \\ +\ 42 \\ \hline \end{array} \qquad \begin{array}{r} 56 \\ -\ 29 \\ \hline \end{array} \qquad \begin{array}{r} 67 \\ +\ 33 \\ \hline \end{array}$$

$$\begin{array}{r} 72 \\ +\ 19 \\ \hline \end{array} \qquad \begin{array}{r} 87 \\ -\ 58 \\ \hline \end{array} \qquad \begin{array}{r} 93 \\ -\ 89 \\ \hline \end{array} \qquad \begin{array}{r} 54 \\ +\ 27 \\ \hline \end{array}$$

The soccer team scored 83 goals this year. The soccer team scored 68 goals last year. How many goals did they score in all?

_____

Directions: Write this number on the blank:

four hundred thousands
five ten thousands
one thousand
eight hundreds
three tens
three ones

_____ _____ _____ , _____ _____ _____

Directions: Add or subtract. Use regrouping when needed.

```
   87        45        95        32
 - 18      + 29      - 27      + 19
```

```
   86        66        74        92
 - 59      - 39      + 23      - 67
```

57 + 18 = _____   42 - 33 = _____   35 + 19 = _____

Sue won 75 tennis games. Jim won 59 tennis games. How many more games did Sue win? _____

Addition: Regrouping

Directions: Study the example. Add using regrouping.

Example:

Add the ones. Regroup.	Add the tens. Regroup.	Add the hundreds.

$$\begin{array}{r} 1 \\ 156 \\ +267 \\ \hline 3 \end{array} \qquad \begin{array}{r} 6 \\ +7 \\ \hline 13 \end{array}$$

$$\begin{array}{r} 11 \\ 156 \\ +267 \\ \hline 23 \end{array} \qquad \begin{array}{r} 1 \\ 5 \\ +6 \\ \hline 12 \end{array}$$

$$\begin{array}{r} 1 \\ 156 \\ +267 \\ \hline 423 \end{array}$$

$$\begin{array}{r} 273 \\ +198 \\ \hline \end{array} \qquad \begin{array}{r} 655 \\ +297 \\ \hline \end{array} \qquad \begin{array}{r} 783 \\ +148 \\ \hline \end{array} \qquad \begin{array}{r} 385 \\ +169 \\ \hline \end{array}$$

$$\begin{array}{r} 29 \\ 46 \\ +12 \\ \hline \end{array} \qquad \begin{array}{r} 81 \\ 78 \\ +33 \\ \hline \end{array} \qquad \begin{array}{r} 52 \\ 67 \\ +23 \\ \hline \end{array} \qquad \begin{array}{r} 49 \\ 37 \\ +19 \\ \hline \end{array}$$

Sally went bowling. She had scores of 115, 129, and 103. What was her total score for three games? _____

Addition: Regrouping

Directions: Add using regrouping. Then, use the code to discover the name of a United States president. The first one is done for you.

```
  348        642        386        184        578
+ 752      + 277      + 787      + 875      + 874
-----
1,100
```

```
  653        653        946        393        199
+ 768      + 359      + 239      + 257      + 843
```

```
  721
+ 679
```

G. ___ ___ ___ ___ ___ ___ ___ ___ ___ ___

1012	1173	1059	1421	919	650	1452	1042	1100	1400	1185
N	A	S	I	W	T	H	O	G	N	G

Addition: Regrouping

Directions: Study the example. Add using regrouping.

Example:

Steps:

```
  5,356      1. Add the ones.
+ 3,976      2. Regroup the tens. Add the tens.
 -------     3. Regroup the hundreds. Add the hundreds.
  9,332      4. Add the thousands.
```

```
  6,849          1,846          9,221
+ 3,276        + 8,384        + 6,769
```

```
  2,758          5,299          7,932
+ 3,663        + 8,764        + 6,879
```

A plane flew 1,838 miles on the first day. It flew 2,347 miles on the second day. How many miles did it fly in all?

_____

Addition: Mental Math

Directions: Try to do these addition problems in your head.

$$\begin{array}{r} 7 \\ +\ 4 \\ \hline \end{array} \qquad \begin{array}{r} 6 \\ +\ 3 \\ \hline \end{array} \qquad \begin{array}{r} 8 \\ +\ 1 \\ \hline \end{array} \qquad \begin{array}{r} 10 \\ +\ 2 \\ \hline \end{array} \qquad \begin{array}{r} 2 \\ +\ 9 \\ \hline \end{array}$$

$$\begin{array}{r} 10 \\ +\ 20 \\ \hline \end{array} \qquad \begin{array}{r} 40 \\ +\ 20 \\ \hline \end{array} \qquad \begin{array}{r} 80 \\ +\ 100 \\ \hline \end{array} \qquad \begin{array}{r} 60 \\ +\ 30 \\ \hline \end{array} \qquad \begin{array}{r} 50 \\ +\ 70 \\ \hline \end{array}$$

$$\begin{array}{r} 350 \\ +\ 150 \\ \hline \end{array} \qquad \begin{array}{r} 300 \\ +\ 500 \\ \hline \end{array} \qquad \begin{array}{r} 400 \\ +\ 800 \\ \hline \end{array} \qquad \begin{array}{r} 450 \\ +\ 10 \\ \hline \end{array} \qquad \begin{array}{r} 680 \\ +\ 100 \\ \hline \end{array}$$

$$\begin{array}{r} 1,000 \\ +\ 200 \\ \hline \end{array} \qquad \begin{array}{r} 4,000 \\ 400 \\ +\ 30 \\ \hline \end{array} \qquad \begin{array}{r} 300 \\ 200 \\ +\ 80 \\ \hline \end{array} \qquad \begin{array}{r} 8,000 \\ 500 \\ +\ 60 \\ \hline \end{array} \qquad \begin{array}{r} 9,800 \\ +\ 150 \\ \hline \end{array}$$

Directions: Regrouping for subtraction is the opposite of regrouping for addition. Study the example. Subtract using regrouping. Then, use the code to color the flowers.

Example:

647
− 453
─────
194

Steps:
1. Subtract the ones.
2. Subtract the tens. Five tens cannot be subtracted from four tens.
3. Regroup the tens by regrouping six hundreds (five hundreds + 10 tens).
4. Add the 10 tens to the four tens.
5. Subtract five tens from 14 tens.
6. Subtract the hundreds.

If the answer has:
one one, color it **red**;
eight ones, color it pink;
five ones, color it yellow.

428
− 397

368
− 173

943
− 652

637
− 242

726
− 331

549
− 361

749
− 568

528
− 270

Subtraction: Regrouping

Directions: Study the example. Follow the steps. Subtract using regrouping.

Example:

Steps:

```
  634
- 455
  179
```

1. Subtract the ones. You cannot subtract five ones from four ones.
2. Regroup the ones by regrouping three tens to two tens + 10 ones.
3. Subtract five ones from 14 ones.
4. Regroup the tens by regrouping the hundreds (five hundreds + 10 tens).
5. Subtract five tens from 12 tens.
6. Subtract the hundreds.

635 − 169	553 − 174	832 − 563	944 − 578
423 − 268	941 − 872	733 − 498	266 − 197
387 − 198	594 − 384	960 − 759	887 − 598

Sophie goes to school 185 days a year. Yoko goes to school 313 days a year. How many more days of school does Yoko attend each year? _____

Directions: Study the example. Follow the steps. Subtract using regrouping. If you have to regroup to subtract ones and there are no tens, you must regroup twice.

Example:

$$
\begin{array}{r}
300 \\
-\ 182 \\
\hline
118
\end{array}
$$

Steps:
1. Subtract the ones. You cannot subtract two ones from zero ones.
2. Regroup. No tens. Regroup the hundreds (two hundreds + 10 tens).
3. Regroup the tens (nine tens + 10 ones).
4. Subtract two ones from 10 ones.
5. Subtract eight tens from nine tens.
6. Subtract one hundred from two hundreds.

$$
\begin{array}{r}
602 \\
-\ 423 \\
\hline
\end{array}
\qquad
\begin{array}{r}
306 \\
-\ 128 \\
\hline
\end{array}
\qquad
\begin{array}{r}
600 \\
-\ 263 \\
\hline
\end{array}
\qquad
\begin{array}{r}
807 \\
-\ 499 \\
\hline
\end{array}
$$

$$
\begin{array}{r}
800 \\
-\ 557 \\
\hline
\end{array}
\qquad
\begin{array}{r}
206 \\
-\ 137 \\
\hline
\end{array}
\qquad
\begin{array}{r}
400 \\
-\ 224 \\
\hline
\end{array}
\qquad
\begin{array}{r}
508 \\
-\ 379 \\
\hline
\end{array}
$$

$$
\begin{array}{r}
207 \\
-\ 138 \\
\hline
\end{array}
\qquad
\begin{array}{r}
604 \\
-\ 397 \\
\hline
\end{array}
\qquad
\begin{array}{r}
308 \\
-\ 199 \\
\hline
\end{array}
\qquad
\begin{array}{r}
700 \\
-\ 531 \\
\hline
\end{array}
$$

Directions: Subtract. Regroup when necessary. The first one is done for you.

7,354	4,214	8,437	6,837
– 5,295	– 3,185	– 5,338	– 4,318
2,059			

5,735	1,036	6,735	3,841
– 3,826	– 947	– 6,646	– 1,953

Columbus discovered America in 1492. The pilgrims landed in America in 1620. How many years difference was there between these two events?

_____

Directions: Try to do these subtraction problems in your head.

9	12	7	5	15
− 3	− 6	− 6	− 1	− 5

40	90	100	20	60
− 20	− 80	− 50	− 20	− 10

450	500	250	690	320
− 250	− 300	− 20	− 100	− 20

1,000	8,000	7,000	4,000	9,500
− 400	− 500	− 900	− 2,000	− 4,000

Review

Directions: Add or subtract using regrouping.

28	82	33	67
56	49	75	94
+ 93	+ 51	+ 128	+ 248

683	756	818	956
− 495	+ 139	− 387	+ 267

1,588	4,675	8,732	2,938
− 989	− 2,976	− 5,664	+ 3,459

The drive from New York City to Los Angeles is 2,832 miles. The drive from New York City to Miami is 1,327 miles. How much farther is it to drive from New York City to Los Angeles than from New York City to Miami?

_____

If the ones number is 5 or greater, round up to the nearest 10. If the ones number is 4 or less, the tens number stays the same and the ones number becomes a zero.

Examples:

15 round up to 20 23 round down to 20 47 round up to 50

Directions: Round these numbers to the nearest ten.

7 _____   58 _____

12 _____   81 _____

33 _____   94 _____

27 _____   44 _____

73 _____   88 _____

25 _____   66 _____

39 _____   70 _____

Rounding: The Nearest Hundred

If the tens number is 5 or greater, round up to the nearest hundred. If the tens number is 4 or less, the hundreds number remains the same.

Remember, look at the number directly to the right of the place you are rounding to.

Examples:

230 round <u>down</u> to 200   470 round up to 500

150 round up to 200   732 round <u>down</u> to 700

Directions: Round these numbers to the nearest hundred.

456 _____   120 _____

340 _____   923 _____

867 _____   550 _____

686 _____   231 _____

770 _____   492 _____

Estimation is useful when you don't need to know the exact amount, but a close answer will do.

When we use estimation, we use only the first number after we round the number up or down. Then, add the numbers together to get the estimate.

Example:

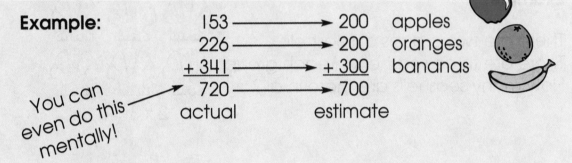

```
 153  ──────►  200    apples
 226  ──────►  200    oranges
+341  ──────► +300    bananas
 720  ──────►  700
actual         estimate
```

You can even do this mentally!

Directions: Estimate the sum of these numbers.

```
 456  ──►
 121  ──►
+438  ──► +  ____
          [    ]
```

```
 910  ──►
 280  ──►
+320  ──► +  ____
          [    ]
```

```
 686  ──►
 307  ──►
+711  ──► +  ____
          [    ]
```

Multiplication

Multiplication is a short way to find the sum of adding the same number a certain amount of times. For example, we write 7 x 4 = 28 instead of 7 + 7 + 7 + 7 = 28.

Directions: Study the example. Multiply.

Example:

There are two groups of seashells.
There are three seashells in each group.
How many seashells are there in all?

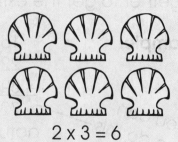

2 x 3 = 6

4 + 4 = _____   3 + 3 + 3 = _____

2 x 4 = _____   3 x 3 = _____

2	3	4	6	7
x 3	x 5	x 3	x 2	x 3

5	6	4	7	8
x 2	x 3	x 2	x 2	x 3

Directions: Multiply.

```
  3          4          3
x 5        x 6        x 8
```

```
  5          4          5
x 5        x 8        x 4
```

```
  6          3          2          7          9
x 7        x 9        x 8        x 6        x 4
```

```
  6          5          7          5          8
x 8        x 6        x 7        x 3        x 9
```

A river boat makes three trips a day every day.
How many trips does it make in a week? _____

Factors are the numbers multiplied together in a multiplication problem. The answer is called the **product**. If you change the order of the factors, the product stays the same.

Example:

There are four groups of fish.
There are three fish in each group.
How many fish are there in all?

$$4 \quad x \quad 3 \quad = \quad 12$$
factor x factor = product

Directions: Draw three groups of four fish.

$3 \times 4 = 12$

Compare your drawing and answer with the example. What did you notice?

Directions: Fill in the missing numbers. Multiply.

$5 \times 4 = $ _____ $3 \times 6 = $ _____ $4 \times 2 = $ _____

$4 \times 5 = $ _____ $6 \times 3 = $ _____ $2 \times 4 = $ _____

$$\begin{array}{r} 3 \\ \times 7 \\ \hline \end{array} \qquad \begin{array}{r} 7 \\ \times 3 \\ \hline \end{array} \qquad \begin{array}{r} 2 \\ \times 9 \\ \hline \end{array} \qquad \begin{array}{r} 9 \\ \times 2 \\ \hline \end{array} \qquad \begin{array}{r} 8 \\ \times 4 \\ \hline \end{array}$$

Any number multiplied by zero equals zero. One multiplied by any number equals that number.

Example:

How many full sails are there in all?

2 boats x **1** sail on each boat = **2** sails

How many full sails are there now?

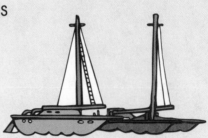

2 boats x **0** sails = **0** sails

Directions: Multiply.

1	2	3	4	0
x 5	x 1	x 0	x 1	x 6

9	8	3	4	7
x 1	x 0	x 1	x 0	x 1

Directions: Time yourself as you multiply. How quickly can you complete this page?

$$\begin{array}{r} 3 \\ \times 2 \\ \hline \end{array} \qquad \begin{array}{r} 8 \\ \times 7 \\ \hline \end{array} \qquad \begin{array}{r} 1 \\ \times 0 \\ \hline \end{array} \qquad \begin{array}{r} 1 \\ \times 6 \\ \hline \end{array} \qquad \begin{array}{r} 3 \\ \times 4 \\ \hline \end{array}$$

$$\begin{array}{r} 4 \\ \times 1 \\ \hline \end{array} \qquad \begin{array}{r} 4 \\ \times 4 \\ \hline \end{array} \qquad \begin{array}{r} 2 \\ \times 5 \\ \hline \end{array} \qquad \begin{array}{r} 9 \\ \times 3 \\ \hline \end{array} \qquad \begin{array}{r} 9 \\ \times 9 \\ \hline \end{array}$$

$$\begin{array}{r} 0 \\ \times 8 \\ \hline \end{array} \qquad \begin{array}{r} 2 \\ \times 6 \\ \hline \end{array} \qquad \begin{array}{r} 9 \\ \times 6 \\ \hline \end{array} \qquad \begin{array}{r} 8 \\ \times 5 \\ \hline \end{array} \qquad \begin{array}{r} 7 \\ \times 3 \\ \hline \end{array}$$

$$\begin{array}{r} 3 \\ \times 5 \\ \hline \end{array} \qquad \begin{array}{r} 2 \\ \times 0 \\ \hline \end{array} \qquad \begin{array}{r} 4 \\ \times 6 \\ \hline \end{array} \qquad \begin{array}{r} 1 \\ \times 3 \\ \hline \end{array} \qquad \begin{array}{r} 0 \\ \times 0 \\ \hline \end{array}$$

Multiplication Table

Directions: Complete the multiplication table. Use it to practice your multiplication facts.

x	0	1	2	3	4	5	6	7	8	9	10
0	0										
1		1									
2			4								
3				9							
4					16						
5						25					
6							36				
7								49			
8									64		
9										81	
10											100

Division is a way to find out how many times one number is contained in another number. For example, $28 \div 4 = 7$ means that there are seven groups of four in 28.

Directions: Study the example. Divide.

Example:

There are six oars.
Each canoe needs two oars.
How many canoes can be used?

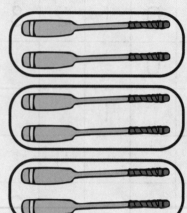

Circle groups of two.
There are three groups of two.

6	÷	2	=	3
oars	÷	numbers	=	canoes
		of oars		
		needed		
		per canoe		

$9 \div 3 =$ _____ $8 \div 2 =$ _____ $16 \div 4 =$ _____

$15 \div 5 =$ _____ $18 \div 2 =$ _____ $20 \div 4 =$ _____

$21 \div 7 =$ _____ $24 \div 6 =$ _____ $12 \div 2 =$ _____

Directions: Divide. Draw a line from the boat to the sail with the correct answer. The first one is done for you.

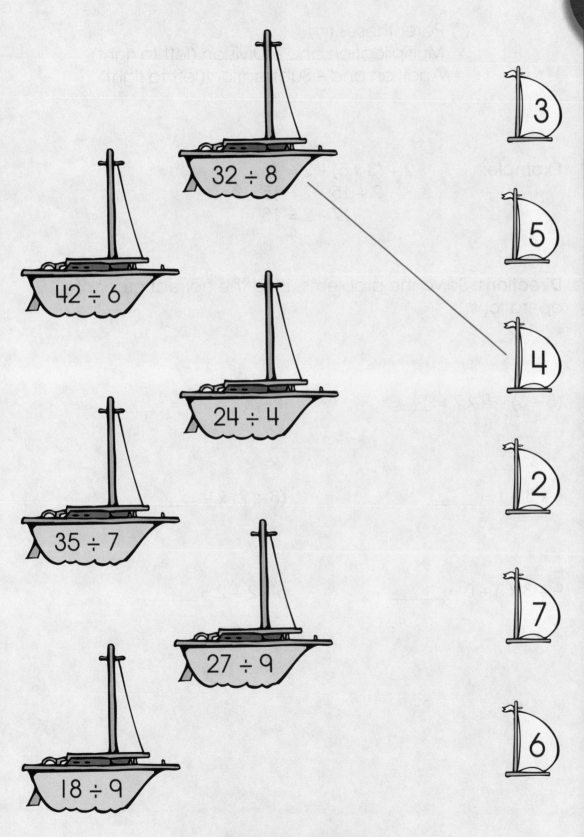

32 ÷ 8

42 ÷ 6

24 ÷ 4

35 ÷ 7

27 ÷ 9

18 ÷ 9

3

5

4

2

7

6

Order of Operations

When you solve a problem that involves more than one operation, this is the order to follow:

( ) Parentheses first
x Multiplication and ÷ Division (left to right)
+ Addition and – Subtraction (left to right)

Example: $2 + (3 \times 5) - 2 = 15$
$2 + 15 - 2 = 15$
$17 - 2 = 15$

Directions: Solve the problems using the correct order of operations.

$(5 - 3) + 4 \times 7 = $ _____ $1 + 2 \times 3 + 4 = $ _____

$6 \times 3 - 1 = $ _____ $(8 \div 2) \times 4 = $ _____

$9 \div 3 \times 3 + 0 = $ _____ $5 - 2 + 2 = $ _____

Directions: Use **+**, **–**, **x**, and **÷** to complete the problems so the number sentence is true.

Example: 4 __+__ 2 __–__ 1 = 5

(8 _____ 2) _____ 4 = 8

(1 _____ 2) _____ 3 = 1

9 _____ 3 _____ 9 = 3

(7 _____ 5) _____ 1 = 2

8 _____ 5 _____ 4 = 10

5 _____ 4 _____ 1 = 1

REMEMBER...
USE THE ORDER OF OPERATIONS

Review

Directions: Multiply or divide. Fill in the blanks with the missing numbers or **x** or ÷ signs. The first one is done for you.

$5 \underline{\ x\ } 4 = 20$ $6 \times 8 = \underline{\hspace{1cm}}$ $7 \times \underline{\hspace{1cm}} = 14$

$3 \underline{\hspace{0.5cm}} 6 = 18$ $7 \times 2 = \underline{\hspace{1cm}}$ $\underline{\hspace{1cm}} \times 3 = 24$

$6 \underline{\hspace{0.5cm}} 2 = 3$ $24 \div 6 = \underline{\hspace{1cm}}$ $6 \times 5 = \underline{\hspace{1cm}}$

$25 \underline{\hspace{0.5cm}} 5 = 5$ $49 \div 7 = \underline{\hspace{1cm}}$ $8 \times \underline{\hspace{1cm}} = 32$

$3 \underline{\hspace{0.5cm}} 8 = 24$ $18 \div 3 = \underline{\hspace{1cm}}$ $9 \times 5 = \underline{\hspace{1cm}}$

$12 \underline{\hspace{0.5cm}} 3 = 4$ $9 \times 8 = \underline{\hspace{1cm}}$ $6 \times \underline{\hspace{1cm}} = 36$

Division

Division is a way to find out how many times one number is contained in another number. The ÷ sign means *divided by*. Another way to divide is to use $\overline{)}$. The **dividend** is the larger number that is divided by the smaller number, or **divisor**. The answer of a division problem is called the **quotient**.

Directions: Study the example. Divide.

Example:

quotient
$$\uparrow$$

20 ÷ 4 = 5

$$\begin{array}{r} 5 \\ 4\overline{)20} \end{array}$$

dividend ↕   divisor ↕   quotient ↕

divisor ↕ dividend ↕

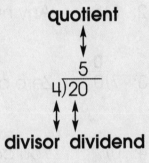

35 ÷ 7 = _____ $7\overline{)35}$ 42 ÷ 6 = _____ $6\overline{)42}$

$2\overline{)12}$ $3\overline{)18}$ $4\overline{)36}$ $5\overline{)50}$

$6\overline{)24}$ $7\overline{)21}$ $8\overline{)32}$ $9\overline{)27}$

36 ÷ 6 = _____   28 ÷ 4 = _____   15 ÷ 5 = _____   12 ÷ 2 = _____

A tree farm has 36 trees. There are four rows of trees. How many trees are there in each row? _____

Division: Zero and One

Directions: Study the rules of division and the examples. Divide, then write the number of the rule you used to solve each problem.

Examples:

Rule 1: $1\overline{)5}$ with 5 above   Any number divided by 1 is that number.

Rule 2: $5\overline{)5}$ with 1 above   Any number except 0 divided by itself is 1.

Rule 3: $7\overline{)0}$ with 0 above   Zero divided by any number is zero.

Rule 4: $0\overline{)7}$ You cannot divide by zero.

$1\overline{)6}$ Rule _____ $1\overline{)7}$ Rule _____

$7\overline{)7}$ Rule _____ $0\overline{)6}$ Rule _____

$9\overline{)0}$ Rule _____ $1\overline{)4}$ Rule _____

Division: Remainders

Division is a way to find out how many times one number is contained in another number. For example, $28 \div 4 = 7$ means that there are seven groups of four in 28. The **dividend** is the larger number that is divided by the smaller number, or **divisor**. The **quotient** is the answer in a division problem. The **remainder** is the amount left over. The remainder is always less than the divisor.

Directions: Study the example. Find each quotient and remainder.

Example:
There are 11 dog biscuits.
Put them in groups of three.
There are two left over.

$$\begin{array}{r} 3 \\ 3\overline{)11} \\ -9 \\ \hline 2 \ \text{remainder} \end{array} \qquad \begin{array}{r} 3\ r2 \\ 3\overline{)11} \end{array}$$

Remember: The remainder must be less than the **divisor**!

$3\overline{)13}$ $\qquad$ $4\overline{)17}$ $\qquad$ $6\overline{)32}$ $\qquad$ $5\overline{)26}$

$9 \div 4 =$ _____ $\qquad$ $12 \div 5 =$ _____ $\qquad$ $26 \div 4 =$ _____ $\qquad$ $49 \div 9 =$ _____

The pet store has seven cats. Two cats go in each cage. How many cats are left over? _____

Multiples

Directions: Draw a **red** circle around the numbers that can be divided by 2. We say these are multiples of two.
Draw a **blue X** on the multiples of three.
Draw a **green** square around the multiples of five.
Draw a **yellow** circle around the multiples of ten.

1	2	3	4	5	6	7	8	9	10
11	12	13	14	15	16	17	18	19	20
21	22	23	24	25	26	27	28	29	30
31	32	33	34	35	36	37	38	39	40
41	42	43	44	45	46	47	48	49	50
51	52	53	54	55	56	57	58	59	60
61	62	63	64	65	66	67	68	69	70
71	72	73	74	75	76	77	78	79	80
81	82	83	84	85	86	87	88	89	90
91	92	93	94	95	96	97	98	99	100

Look at your chart. Common multiples are those which are shared. You have marked them in more than one color. What numbers have all the colors?

Divisibility Rules

A number is divisible...

      by 2 if the last digit is 0 or even (2, 4, 6, 8).
      by 3 if the sum of all digits is divisible by 3.
      by 4 if the last two digits are divisible by 4.
      by 5 if the last digit is a 0 or 5.
      by 10 if the last digit is 0.

Example: 250 is divisible by <u>2, 5, 10</u>

Directions: Look at the numbers below. Tell if the number is divisible by 2, 3, 4, 5, or 10 using the key above.

3,732 _____   439 _____

50 _____   444 _____

7,960 _____   8,212 _____

104,924 _____   2,345 _____

Factor Trees

Factors are the smaller numbers multiplied together to make a larger number. Factor trees are one way to find all the factors of a number.

Example:

Percentages

A **percentage** is the amount of a number out of 100. This is the percent sign: %.

Directions: Fill in the blanks. The first one is done for you.

$70\% = \dfrac{70}{100}$ $\underline{\hspace{1cm}}\% = \dfrac{40}{100}$

$30\% = \dfrac{}{100}$ $10\% = \dfrac{}{100}$

$90\% = \dfrac{}{100}$ $40\% = \dfrac{}{100}$

$70\% = \dfrac{}{100}$ $80\% = \dfrac{}{100}$

$\underline{\hspace{1cm}}\% = \dfrac{20}{100}$ $\underline{\hspace{1cm}}\% = \dfrac{60}{100}$

$\underline{\hspace{1cm}}\% = \dfrac{30}{100}$ $\underline{\hspace{1cm}}\% = \dfrac{10}{100}$

$\underline{\hspace{1cm}}\% = \dfrac{50}{100}$ $\underline{\hspace{1cm}}\% = \dfrac{90}{100}$

Fractions

A **fraction** is a number that names part of a whole, such as $\frac{1}{2}$ or $\frac{1}{3}$.

Example:

$\frac{2}{5}$ parts shaded
parts in the whole figure

Directions: Write the fraction that tells what part of each figure is colored. The first one is done for you.

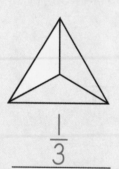

$\frac{1}{3}$
_____

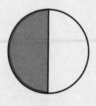

_____

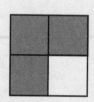

_____

_____

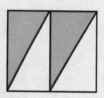

_____

_____

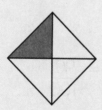

_____

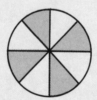

_____

_____

Directions: We often use fractions in cooking or baking. Look for fractions you know as you use this recipe with your mom or dad.

Chocolate Chip Cookies

⭐ **Cream:** 1 cup shortening   1 cup brown sugar

$\frac{1}{2}$ cup sugar   1 teaspoon vanilla

⭐ **Add:** 2 eggs, one at a time. Beat well after each egg is added.

⭐ **Sift:** $2\frac{1}{4}$ cups flour   1 teaspoon salt

1 teaspoon baking soda

Add sifted ingredients to creamed mixture.

⭐ **Stir:** in 2 cups of chocolate chips

⭐ **Bake:** at 350 degrees in an oven for 10 minutes on ungreased cookie sheets

Challenge: Double the recipe and see what happens to the fractions!

Fractions: Equivalent

Fractions that name the same part of a whole are **equivalent fractions**.

Example:

$$\frac{1}{2} = \frac{2}{4}$$

Directions: Fill in the numbers to complete the equivalent fractions.

$$\frac{1}{4} = \frac{\boxed{}}{8}$$

$$\frac{2}{3} = \frac{\boxed{}}{6}$$

$$\frac{1}{6} = \frac{\boxed{}}{12}$$

$$\frac{2}{3} = \frac{\boxed{}}{6}$$

$$\frac{1}{3} = \frac{\boxed{}}{12}$$

$$\frac{1}{5} = \frac{\boxed{}}{15}$$

$$\frac{1}{4} = \frac{\boxed{}}{8}$$

$$\frac{1}{2} = \frac{\boxed{}}{6}$$

$$\frac{2}{3} = \frac{\boxed{}}{9}$$

$$\frac{2}{6} = \frac{\boxed{}}{18}$$

Fractions: Division

A fraction is a number that names part of an object. It can also name part of a group.

Directions: Study the example. Divide by the bottom number of the fraction to find the answers.

Example:
There are six cheerleaders.
$\frac{1}{2}$ of the cheerleaders are boys.
How many cheerleaders are boys?

6 cheerleaders ÷ 2 groups = 3 boys

$\frac{1}{2}$ of 6 = 3

$\frac{1}{2}$ of 10 = _____ $\frac{1}{3}$ of 9 = _____ $\frac{1}{5}$ of 10 = _____

$\frac{1}{4}$ of 12 = _____ $\frac{1}{8}$ of 32 = _____ $\frac{1}{3}$ of 27 = _____

$\frac{1}{5}$ of 30 = _____ $\frac{1}{2}$ of 14 = _____ $\frac{1}{9}$ of 18 = _____

Fractions: Comparing

Directions: Circle the fraction in each pair that is larger.

Example:

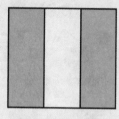

$\left(\dfrac{2}{3}\right)$

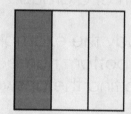

$\dfrac{1}{3}$

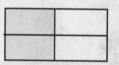

$\dfrac{2}{4}$

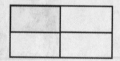

$\dfrac{1}{4}$

$\dfrac{1}{8}$

$\dfrac{2}{8}$

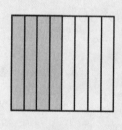

$\dfrac{1}{2}$

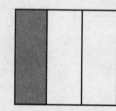

$\dfrac{1}{3}$

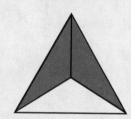

$\dfrac{2}{3}$

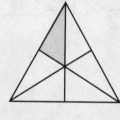

$\dfrac{1}{6}$

$\dfrac{1}{4}$ or $\dfrac{1}{6}$ $\dfrac{1}{5}$ or $\dfrac{1}{7}$ $\dfrac{1}{8}$ or $\dfrac{1}{4}$

Directions: Divide. Draw a line from each problem to the correct answer. The first one is done for you.

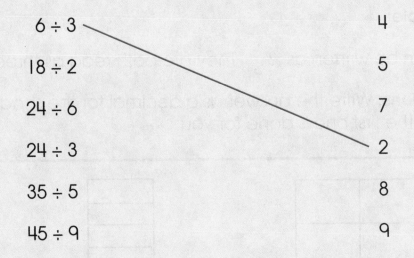

$6 \div 3$

$18 \div 2$

$24 \div 6$

$24 \div 3$

$35 \div 5$

$45 \div 9$

4

5

7

2

8

9

Directions: Divide.

$\frac{1}{3}$ of 12 = _____ $\frac{1}{4}$ of 20 = _____ $\frac{1}{5}$ of 15 = _____

Directions: Color parts of each object to match the fractions given.

$\frac{1}{3}$

$\frac{2}{4}$

$\frac{4}{6}$

$\frac{3}{4}$

Decimals

A **decimal** is a number with one or more numbers to the right of a decimal point. A **decimal point** is a dot placed between the ones place and the tens place of a number, such as 2.5.

Example:

$\frac{3}{10}$ can be written as .3   They are both read as three-tenths.

Directions: Write the answer as a decimal for the shaded parts. The first one is done for you.

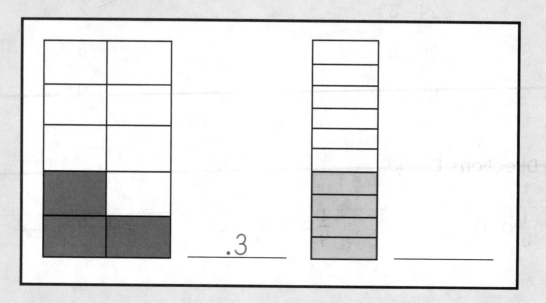

.3

Directions: Color parts of each object to match the decimals given.

.6

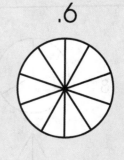

.7

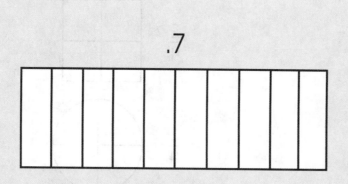

.5

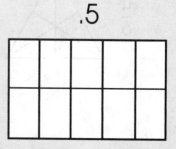

A decimal is a number with one or more numbers to the right of a decimal point, such as 6.5 or 2.25. Equivalent means numbers that are equal.

Directions: Draw a line between the equivalent numbers. The first one is done for you.

.8 $\dfrac{5}{10}$

five-tenths $\dfrac{8}{10}$

.7 $\dfrac{6}{10}$

.4   .3

six-tenths $\dfrac{2}{10}$

three-tenths $\dfrac{7}{10}$

.2 $\dfrac{9}{10}$

nine-tenths $\dfrac{4}{10}$

Decimals Greater Than 1

Directions: Write the decimal for the part that is shaded.

Example: $2\frac{4}{10}$

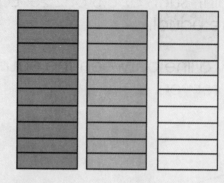

Write: 2.4   **Read:** two and four-tenths

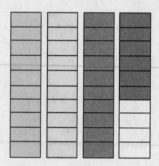

$1\frac{2}{10} =$ _____

$3\frac{6}{10} =$ _____

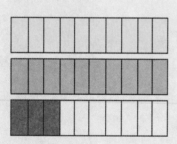

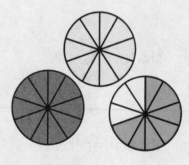

$2\frac{3}{10} =$ _____

$2\frac{7}{10} =$ _____

Directions: Write each number as a decimal.

four and two-tenths = _____   seven and one-tenth = _____

$3\frac{4}{10} =$ _____ $6\frac{9}{10} =$ _____ $8\frac{3}{10} =$ _____

Decimals are added and subtracted in the same way as other numbers. Simply carry down the decimal point to your answer.

Examples:

$$\begin{array}{r} 1 \\ 1.3 \\ +\ 2.8 \\ \hline 4.1 \end{array} \qquad \begin{array}{r} 4.5 \\ -\ 2.2 \\ \hline 2.3 \end{array}$$

Directions: Add or subtract.

$$\begin{array}{r} 1.3 \\ +\ 2.2 \\ \hline \end{array} \qquad \begin{array}{r} 4.6 \\ -\ 3.4 \\ \hline \end{array} \qquad \begin{array}{r} 5.1 \\ +\ 8.8 \\ \hline \end{array} \qquad \begin{array}{r} 6.7 \\ -\ 4.3 \\ \hline \end{array}$$

$$\begin{array}{r} 7.9 \\ -\ 3.7 \\ \hline \end{array} \qquad \begin{array}{r} 6.4 \\ +\ 8.7 \\ \hline \end{array} \qquad \begin{array}{r} 11.4 \\ -\ 9.5 \\ \hline \end{array} \qquad \begin{array}{r} 0.5 \\ +\ 3.6 \\ \hline \end{array}$$

$9.3 + 1.2 =$ _____ $2.5 - 0.7 =$ _____ $1.2 + 5.0 =$ _____

Jacob jogs around the school every day. The distance for one time around is 0.7 of a mile. If he jogs around the school two times, how many miles does he jog each day? _____

Patterns

Directions: Write the one that would come next in each pattern.

0 2 0 4 0 6 _____

1 3 5 7 9 11 _____

5 10 20 40 80 _____

▽ □ ▷ ▭ ▽ □ _____

○ ◯ ● ⬤ ○ ◯ _____

1 A 2 B 3 C _____

A A 1 B B 2 _____

⊞ ⊞ ⊞ ⊞ ⊞ ⊞ _____

Pattern Maze

Directions: Follow the pattern: ● ■ ▲ ☆ to get through the maze.

START

FINISH

Geometry

Geometry is the branch of mathematics that has to do with points, lines, and shapes.

 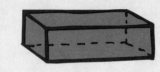 

cube **rectangular prism** **cone** **cylinder** **sphere**

Directions: Use the code to color the picture.

Code:
cubes — **blue**
rectangular prisms — **red**
cones — **green**
cylinders — yellow
spheres — orange

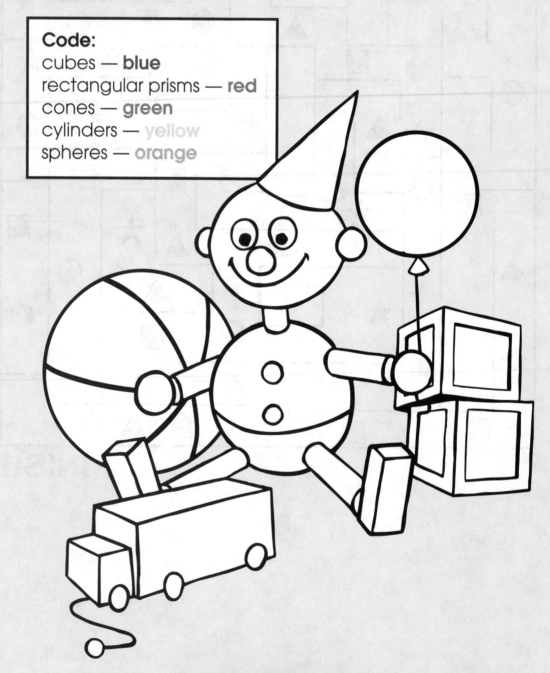

Directions: Cut out the shapes below. Which shapes create a box when folded along the lines?

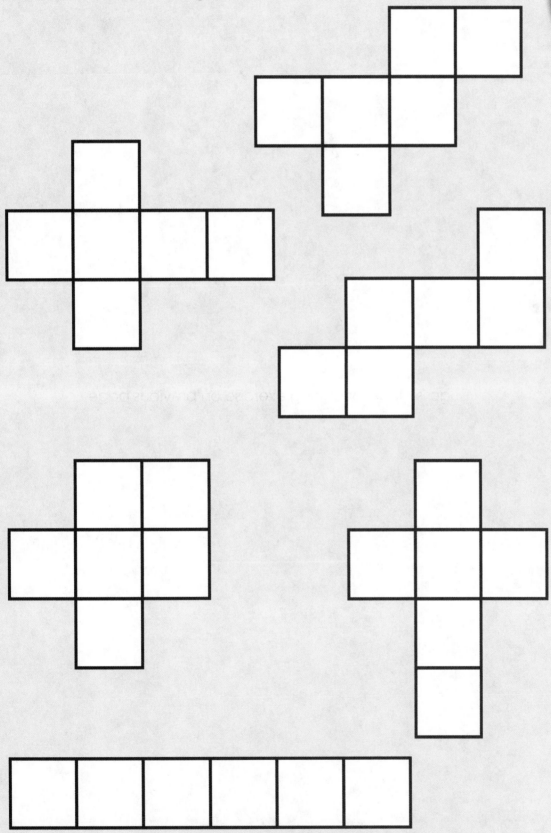

Page is blank for cutting exercise on previous page.

Directions: Cut out the tangram below. Use the shapes to make a cat, a chicken, a boat, and a large triangle.

Page is blank for cutting exercise on previous page.

Directions: 1. Draw four squares.
2. Draw as many possibilities of them touching one edge as you can.

Example:

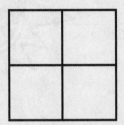 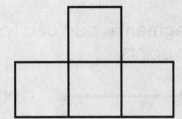

Directions: Count all the triangles.

There are _____ triangles in the figure above.

A **line** goes on and on in both directions. It has no end points.

 Line CD

A **segment** is part of a line. It has two end points.

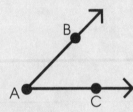 Segment AB

A **ray** has a line segment with only one end point. It goes on and on in the other direction.

 Ray EF

An **angle** has two rays with the same end point.

Angle BAC

Directions: Write the name for each figure. The first one is done for you.

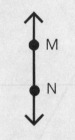

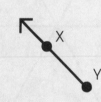

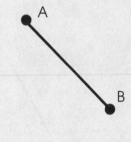

line MN

_____

_____

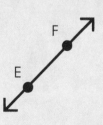

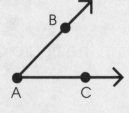

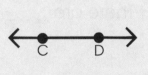

_____

_____

_____

Directions: 1. Cut out the cards at the bottom of the page. Put them in a pile.

2. Cut out the game boards on the next page.

3. Take turns drawing cards.

4. If you have the figure that the card describes on your gameboard, cover it.

5. The first one to get three in a row, wins.

cube	point	cube	cylinder
rectangular prism	line	square	cone
circle	sphere	triangle	segment
rectangle	tangram	ray	

Page is blank for cutting exercise on previous page.

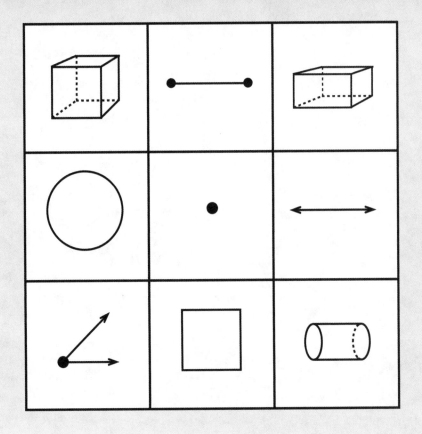

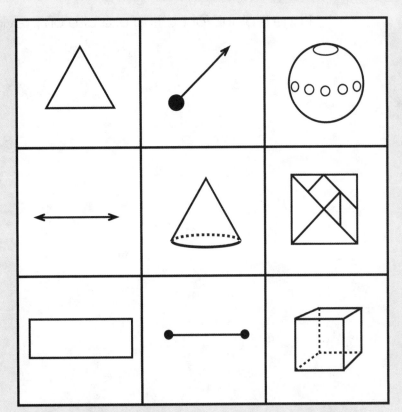

Page is blank for cutting exercise on previous page.

Geometry: Perimeter

The **perimeter** is the distance around an object. Find the perimeter by adding the lengths of all the sides.

Directions: Find the perimeter for each object (ft. = feet). The first one is done for you.

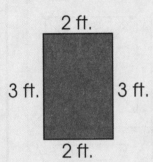 2 ft. / 3 ft. 3 ft. / 2 ft.

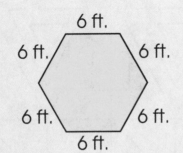 6 ft. 6 ft. 6 ft. 6 ft. 6 ft. 6 ft.

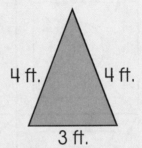 4 ft. 4 ft. 3 ft.

__10 ft.__   _____   _____

10 ft. / 3 ft. 3 ft. / 10 ft.

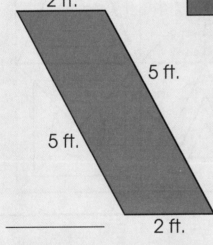 2 ft. 5 ft. 5 ft. 2 ft.

_____

3 ft. / 1 ft. 1 ft. / 5 ft.
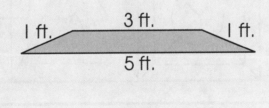
_____

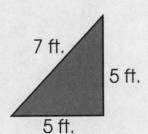 7 ft. 5 ft. 5 ft.

1 ft. 1 ft. 1 ft. 1 ft. 1 ft. 1 ft. 1 ft. 1 ft.

_____   _____

Master Skills Math Grade 3

Geometric Coloring

Directions: Color the geometric shapes in the box below.

Flower Power

Directions: Count the flowers and answer the questions.

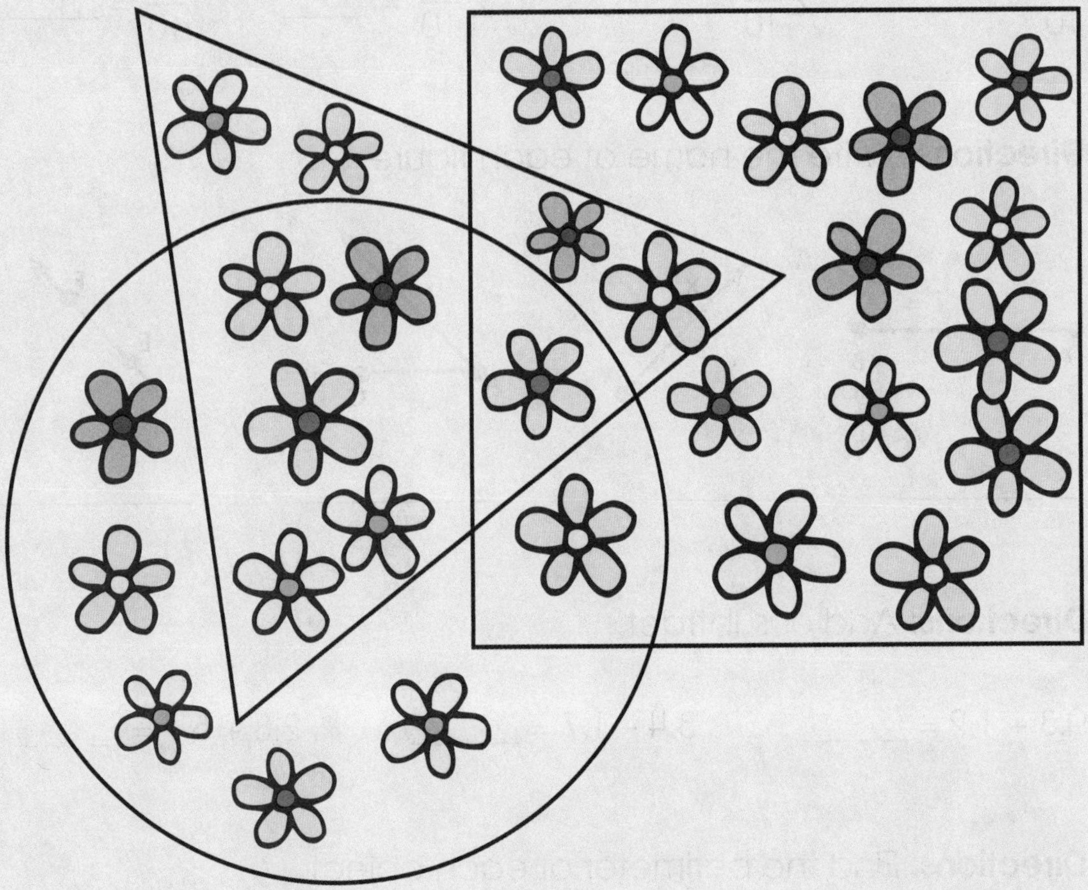

How many 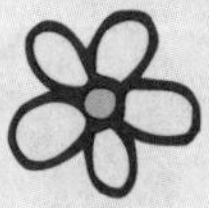 s are in the circle? ______

How many  s are in the triangle? ______

How many  s are in the square? ______

How many 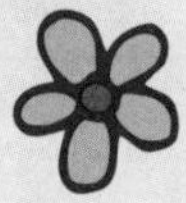 s in all? ______

Directions: Write the decimal for each fraction.

$\frac{3}{10}$ = _____ $2\frac{4}{10}$ = _____ $12\frac{7}{10}$ = _____ $\frac{8}{10}$ = _____

Directions: Write the name of each figure.

   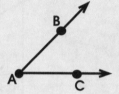

_____   _____   _____   _____

Directions: Add or subtract.

9.3 + 1.2 = _____   3.4 – 1.7 = _____   2.8 + 5.7 = _____

Directions: Find the perimeter of each object.

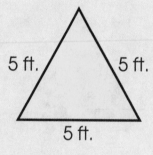   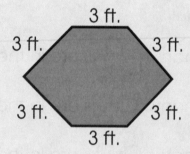

_____   _____

Graphs

A **graph** is a drawing that shows information about numbers.

Directions: Color the picture. Then, tell how many there are of each object by completing the graph.

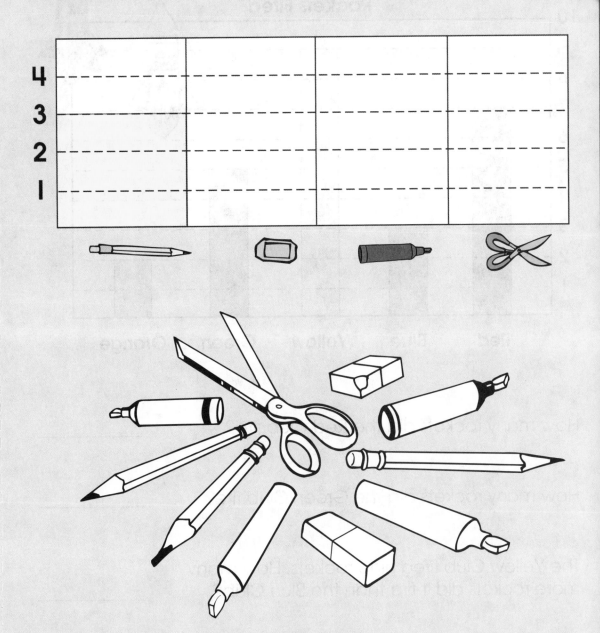

Graphs

Directions: Answer the questions about the graph.

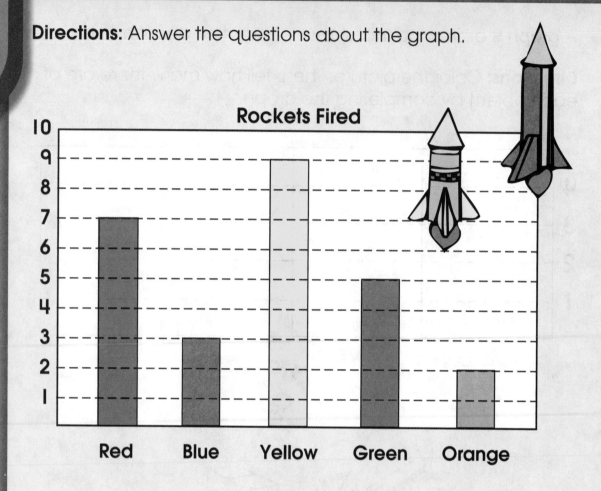

How many rockets did the Red Club fire? _____

How many rockets did the Green Club fire? _____

The Yellow Club fired nine rockets. How many
more rockets did it fire than the Blue Club? _____

How many rockets were fired in all? _____

An **inch** is a unit of length in the standard measurement system.

Directions: Use a ruler to measure each object to the nearest $\frac{1}{4}$ inch. Write **in.** to stand for inch.

Examples:

I in.

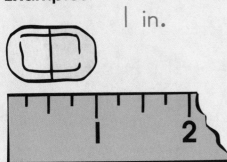

$2\frac{1}{2}$ in.

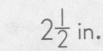

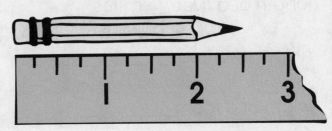

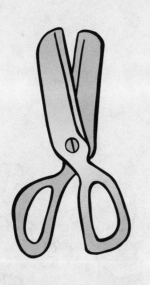

_____   _____

_____

_____

I foot = 12 inches
I yard = 36 inches or 3 feet
I mile = 1,760 yards

Directions: Decide whether you would use foot, yard, or mile to measure each object. The first one is done for you.

length of a river ___miles___

height of a tree _____

width of a room _____

length of a football field _____

height of a door _____

length of a dress _____

length of a race _____

height of a basketball hoop _____

width of a window _____

distance a plane travels _____

Directions: Solve the problem.

Tara races Jacob in the 100-yard dash. Tara finishes 10 yards in front of Jacob. How many feet did Tara finish in front of Jacob? _____

Ounces and **pounds** are measurements of weight in the standard measurement system. The ounce is used to measure the weight of very light objects. The pound is used to measure the weight of heavier objects. **16 ounces = 1 pound**.

Examples:

8 ounces   15 pounds

Directions: Decide if you would use ounces or pounds to measure the weight of each object. Circle your answer.

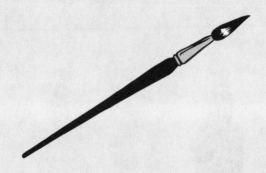

ounce   pound

ounce   pound

ounce   pound

ounce   pound

A **centimeter** is a unit of length in the metric system. There are 2.54 centimeters in an inch.

Directions: Use a centimeter ruler to measure each object to the nearest half of a centimeter. Write **cm** to stand for centimeter.

Examples:

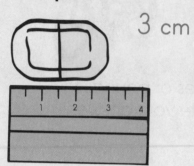

3 cm

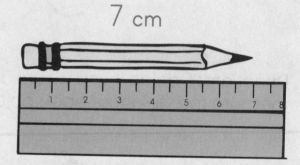

7 cm

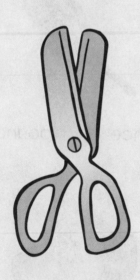

_____

_____   _____

_____

Meters and **kilometers** are units of length in the metric system. A meter is equal to 39.37 inches. A kilometer is equal to about $\frac{5}{8}$ of a mile.

1 meter = 100 centimeters
1 kilometer = 1,000 meters

Directions: Decide whether you would use meter or kilometer to measure each object. The first one is done for you.

length of a river __kilometer__

height of a tree _____

width of a room _____

length of a football field _____

height of a door _____

length of a dress _____

length of a race _____

height of a basketball pole _____

width of a window _____

Directions: Solve the problem.

Sarah races Jon in the 100-meter dash. Sarah finishes 10 meters in front of Jon. How many centimeters did Sarah finish in front of Jon? _____

Directions: Circle the correct answers.

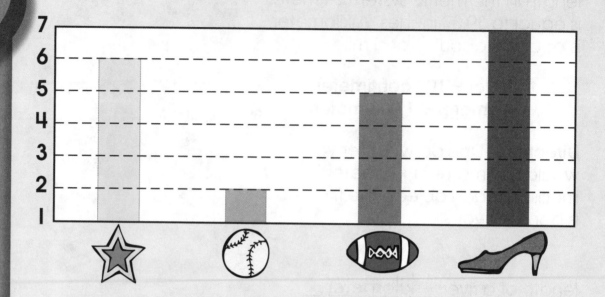

Are there more shoes or stars?	stars	shoes
How many more footballs than baseballs?	2	3
Are there fewer stars or footballs?	stars	footballs

Which would you use to measure...

...a horse?	ounce	pound
...a bird?	ounce	pound
...length of a car?	inches	feet
...width of a river?	inches	yards
...height of a room?	centimeters	meters

Directions: Locate the points on the grid and color in each box.

What animal did you form? _____

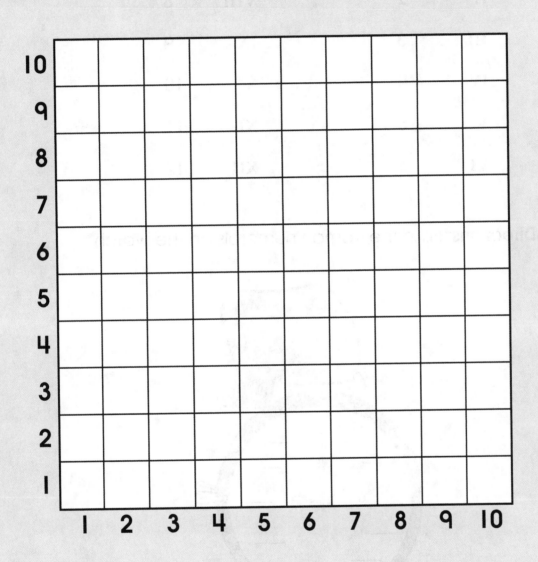

(across, up)

(4, 7)	(4, 1)	(7, 1)	(3, 5)	(2, 8)	(8, 6)	(4, 8)	(3, 7)
(5, 4)	(6, 5)	(5, 5)	(6, 6)	(7, 3)	(8, 5)	(10, 5)	(4, 3)
(7, 6)	(4, 6)	(1, 8)	(6, 4)	(7, 2)	(4, 5)	(9, 6)	(4, 9)
(3, 6)	(7, 5)	(5, 6)	(4, 2)	(4, 4)	(7, 4)	(2, 7)	(3, 8)

Roman Numerals

Another way to write numbers is to use Roman numerals.

I	1	VII	7
II	2	VIII	8
III	3	IX	9
IV	4	X	10
V	5	XI	11
VI	6	XII	12

Directions: Fill in the Roman numerals on the watch.

What time is it on the watch?

_____ o'clock

Roman Numerals

I	1	VII	7
II	2	VIII	8
III	3	IX	9
IV	4	X	10
V	5	XI	11
VI	6	XII	12

Directions: Write the number.

V _____   VII _____

X _____   IX _____

II _____   XII _____

Directions: Write the Roman numeral.

4 _____   5 _____

10 _____   8 _____

6 _____   3 _____

Directions: Write the time shown on each clock.

Examples:

7:15

7:00

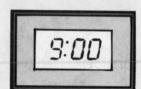

_____

_____

_____

_____

_____

_____

_____

_____

_____

Time: a.m. and p.m.

In telling time, the hours between 12:00 midnight and 12:00 noon are a.m. hours. The hours between 12:00 noon and 12:00 midnight are p.m. hours.

Directions: Draw a line between the times that are the same.

Examples:

7:30 in the morning ————— 7:30 a.m.
half-past seven a.m.
seven thirty in the morning

9:00 in the evening - - - - - - - - - 9:00 p.m.
nine o'clock at night

six o'clock in the evening   8:00 a.m.

3:30 a.m.   six o'clock in the morning

4:15 p.m.   6:00 p.m.

eight o'clock in the   eleven o'clock at night
morning

quarter past five in the   three thirty in the morning
evening

11:00 p.m.   four fifteen in the afternoon

6:00 a.m.   5:15 p.m.

Time: Minutes

A minute is a measurement of time. There are 60 seconds in a minute and 60 minutes in an hour.

Directions: Write the time shown on each clock.

Example:

Each mark is one minute.
The hand is at mark number 6.

Write: 5:06
Read: six minutes after five.

_____

_____

_____

5:38

2:47

_____

_____

_____

3:18

_____

_____

_____

Directions: Add the hours and minutes together.
(Remember, 1 hour equals 60 minutes.)

Examples:

```
  2 hours  10 minutes
+ 1 hour   50 minutes
  3 hours (60 minutes)
        (1 hour)
  4 hours
```

```
  4 hours  20 minutes
+ 2 hours  10 minutes
  6 hours  30 minutes
```

```
  9 hours
+ 2 hours
```

```
  1 hour
+ 5 hours
```

```
  6 hours
+ 3 hours
```

```
  6 hours  15 minutes
+ 1 hour   15 minutes
```

```
  10 hours  30 minutes
+  1 hour   10 minutes
```

```
  3 hours  40 minutes
+ 8 hours  20 minutes
```

```
  11 hours  15 minutes
+  1 hour   30 minutes
```

```
  4 hours  15 minutes
+ 5 hours  45 minutes
```

```
  7 hours  10 minutes
+ 1 hour   30 minutes
```

Time: Subtraction

Directions: Subtract the hours and minutes.
(Remember, 1 hour equals 60 minutes.)
Borrow from the hours if you need to.

Example:

```
   5        70
   6 hours  10 minutes
 - 2 hours  30 minutes
   3 hours  40 minutes
```

```
  12 hours          5 hour           2 hours
 - 2 hours        - 3 hours        - 1 hour
```

```
   5 hours  30 minutes          9 hours  45 minutes
 - 2 hours  15 minutes        - 3 hours  15 minutes
```

```
  11 hours  50 minutes         12 hours
 - 4 hours  35 minutes       - 6 hours  30 minutes
```

```
   7 hours  15 minutes          8 hours  10 minutes
 - 5 hours  30 minutes        - 4 hours  40 minutes
```

 dollar = 100¢ or $1.00

 penny = 1¢ or $.01

 nickel = 5¢ or $.05

 dime = 10¢ or $.10

 quarter = 25¢ or $.25

 half-dollar = 50¢ or $.50

Directions: Write the amount for each group of money shown. Use a dollar sign and decimal point. The first one is done for you.

 $0.07

_____

_____

_____

_____

_____

Money: Five-Dollar Bill and Ten-Dollar Bill

Five-dollar bill =
5 one-dollar bills

Ten-dollar bill =
2 five-dollar bills or
10 one-dollar bills

Directions: Write the amount for each group of money shown. Use a dollar sign and decimal point. The first one is done for you.

$15.00   _____

_____   _____

7 one-dollar bills, 2 quarters _____

2 five-dollar bills, 3 one-dollar bills, half-dollar _____

Money: Counting Change

Directions: Subtract the money using decimals to show how much change a person would receive in each of the following.

Example:
Bill had 3 dollars.
He bought a baseball for $2.83.
How much change did he receive?

$$\begin{array}{r} \$3.00 \\ -\ \$2.83 \\ \hline \$\ .17 \end{array}$$

Paid 2 dollars.

_____

Paid 1 dollar.

_____

Paid 5 dollars.

_____

Paid 10 dollars.

_____

Paid 4 dollars.

_____

Paid 7 dollars.

_____

Money: Comparing

Directions: Compare the amount of money in the left column with the price of the object in the right column. Is the amount of money in the left column enough to purchase the object in the right column? Circle **yes** or **no**.

Yes   No

Yes   No

Yes   No

Yes   No

Directions: Complete each clock to show the time written below it.

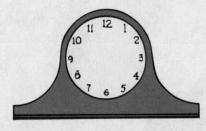

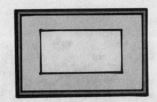

7:15   3:07   6:25

Directions: Write the time using a.m. or p.m.

seven twenty-two in the evening _____

three fifteen in the morning _____

Directions: Write the correct amount of money.

_____   _____

Joey paid $4.67 for a model car. He gave the clerk a five-dollar bill. How much change should he receive?

_____

Problem-Solving:
Addition, Subtraction

Directions: Read and solve each problem. The first one is done for you.

The clown started the day with 200 balloons. He gave away 128 of them. Some broke. At the end of the day, he had 18 balloons left. How many of the balloons broke?

54 balloons

On Monday, there were 925 tickets sold to adults and 1,412 tickets sold to children. How many more children attended the fair than adults?

_____

At one game booth, prizes were given out for scoring 500 points in three attempts. Sydney scored 178 points on her first attempt, 149 points on her second attempt, and 233 points on her third attempt. Did Sydney win a prize?

_____

The prize-winning steer weighed 2,348 pounds. The runner-up steer weighed 2,179 pounds. How much more did the prize steer weigh?

_____

Directions: Read and solve each problem.

Jeff and Terry are planting a garden. They plant three rows of green beans with eight plants in each row. How many green bean plants are there in the garden? _____

There are 45 tomato plants in the garden. There are five rows of them. How many tomato plants are in each row? _____

The children have 12 plants each of lettuce, broccoli, and spinach. How many plants are there in all? _____

Jeff planted three times as many cucumber plants as Terry. He planted 15 of them. How many did Terry plant? _____

Terry planted 12 pepper plants. He planted twice as many green pepper plants as red pepper plants. How many green pepper plants are there? _____

How many red pepper plants? _____

A fraction is a number that names part of a whole, such as $\frac{1}{2}$ or $\frac{1}{3}$.

Directions: Read and solve each problem.

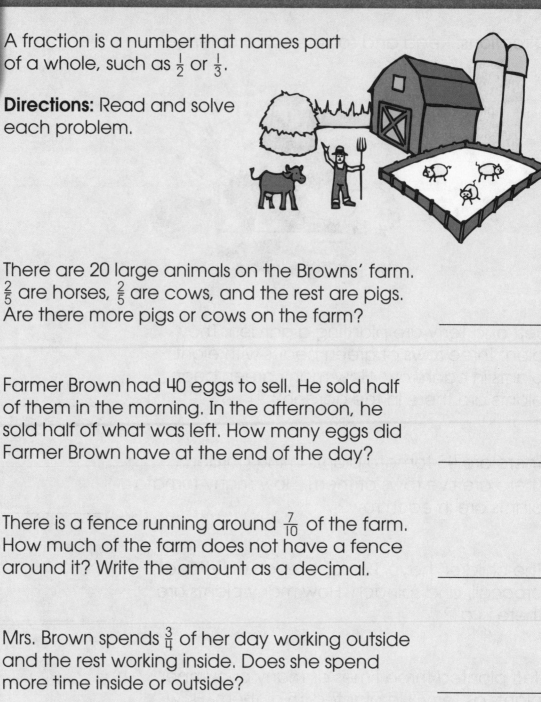

There are 20 large animals on the Browns' farm. $\frac{2}{5}$ are horses, $\frac{2}{5}$ are cows, and the rest are pigs. Are there more pigs or cows on the farm? _____

Farmer Brown had 40 eggs to sell. He sold half of them in the morning. In the afternoon, he sold half of what was left. How many eggs did Farmer Brown have at the end of the day? _____

There is a fence running around $\frac{7}{10}$ of the farm. How much of the farm does not have a fence around it? Write the amount as a decimal. _____

Mrs. Brown spends $\frac{3}{4}$ of her day working outside and the rest working inside. Does she spend more time inside or outside? _____

Directions: Read and solve each problem.

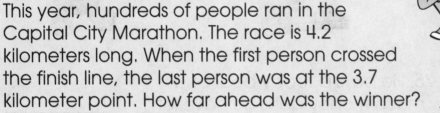

This year, hundreds of people ran in the Capital City Marathon. The race is 4.2 kilometers long. When the first person crossed the finish line, the last person was at the 3.7 kilometer point. How far ahead was the winner? _____

Dennis crossed the finish line 10 meters ahead of Lucy. Lucy was 5 meters ahead of Sam. How far ahead of Sam was Dennis? _____

Tony ran 320 yards from school to his home. Then, he ran 290 yards to Jay's house. Together, Tony and Jay ran 545 yards to the store. How many yards in all did Tony run? _____

The teacher measured the heights of three children in her class. Marsha was 51 inches tall, Jimmy was 48 inches tall, and Ted was $52\frac{1}{2}$ inches tall. How much taller is Ted than Marsha? _____

How much taller is he than Jimmy? _____

Problem-Solving: Measurement

Directions: Read and solve each problem.

Ralph has $8.75. He buys a teddy bear and
a puzzle. How much money does he have left?

_____

Kelly wants to buy a teddy bear and a ball.
She has $7.25. How much more money
does she need?

_____

Kim paid a five-dollar bill, two one-dollar bills,
two quarters, one dime, and eight pennies
for a book. How much did it cost?

_____

Michelle leaves for school at 7:45 a.m.
It takes her 20 minutes to get there.
On the clock, draw the time that she
arrives at school.

Frank takes piano lessons every
Saturday morning at 11:30.
The lesson lasts for an hour and
15 minutes. On the clock, draw
the time his piano lesson ends.
Is it a.m. or p.m.? Circle the
correct answer.

Directions: Read and solve each of the problems.

The baker sets out nine baking pans with six rolls on each one. How many rolls are there in all? _____

A dozen brownies cost $1.29. James pays for a dozen brownies with a five-dollar bill. How much change does he receive? _____

Theresa has four quarters, a nickel, and three pennies. How much more money does she need to buy brownies? _____

The baker made 24 loaves of bread. At the end of the day, he has $\frac{1}{4}$ left. How many did he sell? _____

The bakery opens at 8:30 a.m. It closes nine and a half hours later. What time does it close? _____

Math Terms Crossword

Directions: Use your glossary and the clues on page 99 to help you fill in the words.

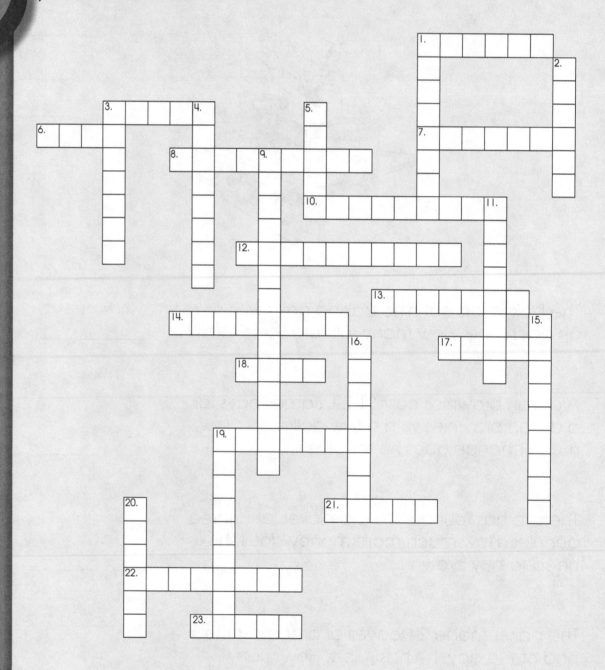

Math Terms Crossword

Across:

1. 100¢

3. Symbols used to write numbers

6. A measurement of distance in the standard measurement system that is equal to 1,760 yards

7. Part of a line with two end points

8. A measurement of distance in the metric system of a great distance

10. A figure with four corners and four sides

12. Answer in a subtraction problem

13. Smaller number that is divided into the dividend

14. Answer of a division problem

17. A measurement of weight in the standard measurement system of a very light object

18. A measurement of distance in the standard measurement system that is equal to 36 inches

19. Answer in a multiplication problem

21. Two rays with the same end point

22. Putting together two or more numbers to find the sum

23. A drawing that shows information about numbers

Down:

1. Operation to find out how many times one number is contained in another

2. A number multiplied together in a problem

3. A number with one or more places to the right

4. A figure with three corners and three sides

5. A measurement of length in the metric system of a short distance

9. A short way to find the sum of adding the same number many times

11. A point at the end of a line segment or ray

15. The number left over in the quotient

16. A number that names part of a whole

19. Distance around an object

20. A figure with four corners and four sides of equal length

Directions: See how many words you can make from the letters in the word **Mathematics**.

Mathematics

_____   _____

_____   _____

_____   _____

_____   _____

_____   _____

_____   _____

For a challenge, time yourself or race another person.

Directions: Write the number's value in each place: **678,421**.

_____ ones   _____ hundred thousands

_____ thousands   _____ hundreds

_____ tens   _____ ten thousands

Directions: Add or subtract. Remember to regroup, if you need to.

$$\begin{array}{r} 88 \\ -19 \\ \hline \end{array} \qquad \begin{array}{r} 46 \\ +39 \\ \hline \end{array} \qquad \begin{array}{r} 75 \\ +24 \\ \hline \end{array} \qquad \begin{array}{r} 93 \\ -68 \\ \hline \end{array}$$

$$\begin{array}{r} 683 \\ -496 \\ \hline \end{array} \qquad \begin{array}{r} 84 \\ 49 \\ +62 \\ \hline \end{array} \qquad \begin{array}{r} 97 \\ 54 \\ +361 \\ \hline \end{array} \qquad \begin{array}{r} 9,731 \\ -4,664 \\ \hline \end{array}$$

Directions: Round to the nearest ten, hundred, or thousand.

72 _____   49 _____   31 _____   66 _____

151 _____   296 _____   917 _____   621 _____

Review

Directions: Multiply or divide.

$$\begin{array}{r} 3 \\ \times 6 \\ \hline \end{array} \qquad \begin{array}{r} 3 \\ \times 8 \\ \hline \end{array} \qquad \begin{array}{r} 9 \\ \times 8 \\ \hline \end{array} \qquad \begin{array}{r} 9 \\ \times 5 \\ \hline \end{array}$$

$$5 \overline{)25} \qquad 2 \overline{)6} \qquad 3 \overline{)18} \qquad 8 \overline{)24}$$

Directions: Divide.

$\dfrac{1}{3}$ of 12 = _____ $\dfrac{1}{7}$ of 28 = _____ $\dfrac{1}{9}$ of 45 = _____

Directions: Color parts to match the fractions given.

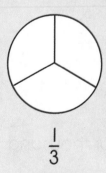

$\dfrac{1}{3}$

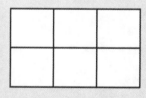

$\dfrac{2}{4}$ $\dfrac{2}{6}$

Directions: Write the decimal for each fraction.

$\frac{4}{10}$ = _____ $3\frac{3}{10}$ = _____ $\frac{9}{10}$ = _____ $21\frac{3}{10}$ = _____

Directions: Add or subtract.

$8.2 + 1.1 =$ _____ $3.6 - 1.8 =$ _____ $3.9 + 2.6 =$ _____

Directions: Write the name for each figure.

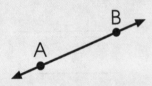      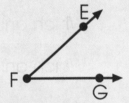

_____   _____   _____   _____

Directions: Find the perimeter of each object.

4 ft.

4 ft. [square] 4 ft.

4 ft.

4 ft.

1 ft. [rectangle] 1 ft.

4 ft.

6 ft. [triangle] 6 ft.

6 ft.

_____   _____   _____

Directions: Answer the questions.

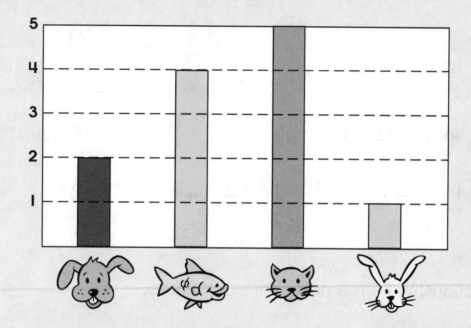

Which animal is there the most of? _____

Which animal is there the fewest of? _____

How many animals altogether? _____

Directions: Answer the questions.

What unit of measure would you use to measure…

...a cow? _____

...a mouse? _____

...length of a pencil? _____

...length of a semi-truck? _____

...length of a river? _____

...width of a river? _____

Directions: Complete each clock to show the time written below it.

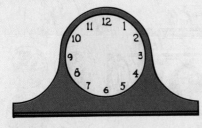

9:00

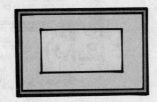

10:15

2:35

Directions: Write the time, using a.m. or p.m.

six twenty-two in the evening _____

nine forty-six in the morning _____

Directions: Add or subtract.

```
  2 hours  15 minutes          1 hour   30 minutes
+ 4 hours  30 minutes        + 4 hours  30 minutes
```

```
 12 hours  45 minutes          8 hours  30 minutes
- 4 hours  30 minutes        - 3 hours  45 minutes
```

Review

Directions: Write the amount of money.

_____   _____

$$
\begin{array}{r}
\$5.00 \\
-\ 4.67 \\
\hline
\end{array}
\qquad
\begin{array}{r}
\$6.51 \\
-\ 2.49 \\
\hline
\end{array}
$$

Directions: Read and solve each problem.

Katarina has 12 pieces of cake. After school, she has $\frac{1}{4}$ of the cake left. How much cake was eaten? _____

Four jars of play dough weigh one pound. How many jars would weigh three pounds? _____

Addition: "Putting together" or adding two or more numbers to find the sum.

Angle: Two rays with the same end point.

Centimeter: A measurement of length in the metric system. There are 2.54 centimeters in an inch.

Decimal: A number with one or more places to the right of a decimal point, such as 6.5 or 3.78. Money amounts are written with two places to the right of a decimal point, such as $1.30.

Difference: The answer in a subtraction problem.

Digit: The symbols used to write numbers: 0, 1, 2, 3, 4, 5, 6, 7, 8, and 9.

Dividend: The larger number that is divided by the smaller number, or divisor, in a division problem. In the problem 28 ÷ 7 = 4, 28 is the dividend.

Division: An operation to find out how many times one number is contained in another number. **Example:** 28 ÷ 4 = 7 means that there are seven groups of four in 28.

Divisor: The smaller number that is divided into the dividend in a division problem. In the problem 28 ÷ 7 = 4, 7 is the divisor.

Dollar: A dollar is equal to one hundred cents. It is written $1.00.

End Point: A point at the end of a line segment or ray.

Factors: The numbers multiplied together in a multiplication problem.

Fraction: A number that names part of a whole, such as $\frac{1}{2}$ or $\frac{1}{3}$.

Geometry: The branch of mathematics that has to do with points, lines, and shapes.

Graph: A drawing that shows information about numbers.

Kilometer: A measurement of distance in the metric system. There are 1,000 meters in a kilometer.

Meter: A measurement of length in the metric system. A meter is equal to 39.37 inches.

Mile: A measurement of distance in the standard measurement system. A mile is equal to 1,760 yards.

Glossary

Multiplication: A short way to find the sum of adding the same number a certain amount of times. For example, 7 x 4 = 28 instead of 7 + 7 + 7 + 7 = 28.

Ounce: A measurement of weight in the standard measurement system. There are 16 ounces in a pound.

Perimeter: The distance around an object. Find the perimeter by adding the lengths of the sides.

Place Value: The value of a digit, or numeral, shown by where it is in the number.

Product: The answer of a multiplication problem.

Quotient: The answer of a division problem.

Ray: A line segment with only one end point. It goes on and on in the other direction.

Rectangle: A figure with four corners and four sides. Sides opposite each other are the same length.

Regroup: To use 10 ones to form one ten, 10 tens to form one hundred, and so on.

Remainder: The number left over in the quotient of a division problem.

Segment: A part of a line with two end points.

Square: A figure with four corners and four sides of the same length.

Subtraction: "Taking away" or subtracting one number from another to find the difference.

Triangle: A figure with three corners and three sides.

Yard: A measurement of distance in the standard measurement system. There are three feet in a yard.

2 — Numbers: Spanish / Los Números en Español

Directions: Match the numbers 1-20. The first one is done for you.

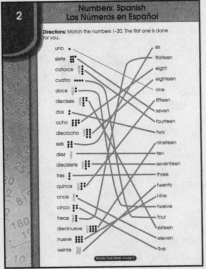

- uno — six
- siete — thirteen
- catorce — eight
- cuatro — eighteen
- doce — one
- dieciséis — fifteen
- dos — seven
- ocho — fourteen
- dieciocho — two
- seis — nineteen
- diez — ten
- diecisiete — seventeen
- tres — three
- quince — twenty
- once — nine
- cinco — twelve
- trece — four
- diecinueve — sixteen
- nueve — eleven
- veinte — five

3 — Addition: Spanish / Add in Spanish!

Addition means "putting together" or adding two or more numbers to find the sum. For example, 3 + 5 = 8.

"Más" means plus in Spanish.

Example: uno más tres = 4
1 + 3

Directions: Add to find the answer.

- siete más catorce = 21
- nueve más veinte = 29
- cuatro más doce = 16
- once más quince = 26
- dieciséis más dos = 18
- ocho más uno = 9
- cinco más tres = 8
- diez más seis = 16
- tres más diez = 13

4 — Addition

Example:

Add the ones.
26
+ 21
7

Add the tens.
26
+ 21
47

Directions: Add.

18 + 11 **29**	24 + 35 **59**	38 + 21 **59**	49 + 50 **99**
75 + 12 **87**	83 + 16 **99**	67 + 32 **99**	44 + 25 **69**

68 + 20 = **88** 54 + 25 = **79**

The Lions scored 42 points. The Clippers scored 21 points. How many points were scored in all? **63 points**

5 — Addition: Football Math

Directions: Follow the plays of your favorite team.

A touchdown is worth 6 points.
A field goal is worth 3 points.

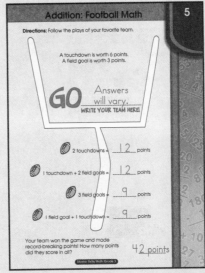

GO Answers will vary. WRITE YOUR TEAM HERE

- 2 touchdowns = **12** points
- 1 touchdown + 2 field goals = **12** points
- 3 field goals = **9** points
- 1 field goal + 1 touchdown = **9** points

Your team won the game and made record-breaking points! How many points did they score in all? **42 points**

6 — Subtraction

Subtraction means "taking away" or subtracting one number from another to find the difference. For example, 10 - 3 = 7.

Example:

Subtract the ones.
39
- 24
5

Subtract the tens.
39
- 24
15

Directions: Subtract.

48 - 35 **13**	95 - 22 **73**	87 - 16 **71**	55 - 43 **12**
37 - 14 **23**	69 - 57 **12**	44 - 23 **21**	99 - 78 **21**

66 - 44 = **22** 57 - 33 = **24**

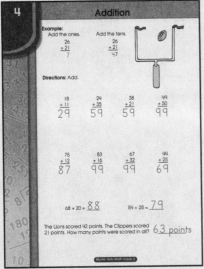

The yellow car traveled 87 miles per hour. The orange car traveled 66 miles per hour. How much faster was the yellow car traveling? **21 m.p.h.**

7 — Place Value

The place value of a digit, or numeral, is shown by where it is in the number. For example, in the number 1,234, 1 has the place value of thousands, 2 is hundreds, 3 is tens, and 4 is ones.

Hundred Thousands	Ten Thousands	Thousands	Hundreds	Tens	Ones
9	4	3	8	5	2

943,852

Directions: Match the numbers in Column A with the words in Column B. The first one is done for you.

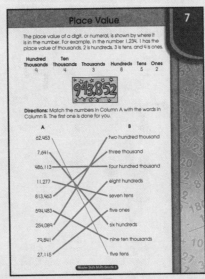

A	B
62,453	two hundred thousand
7,641	three thousand
486,113	four hundred thousand
11,277	eight hundreds
813,463	seven tens
594,483	five ones
254,089	six hundreds
79,841	nine ten thousands
27,115	five tens

Answer Key

8 — Place Value

Directions: Use the code to color the rings.

If the number has:
seven ten thousands, color it red.
one thousand, color it blue.
four hundred thousands, color it green.
six tens, color it brown.
eight ones, color it yellow.

8

9 — Addition: Regrouping

Addition means "putting together" or adding two or more numbers to find the sum. To regroup is to use 10 ones to form one ten, 10 tens to form one hundred, and so on.

Example:

Add the ones.	Add the tens with regrouping.
88 +21 = 9	88 +21 = 109

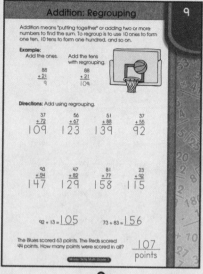

Directions: Add using regrouping.

37 +72 = 109	56 +67 = 123	51 +88 = 139	37 +55 = 92

93 +54 = 147	47 +82 = 129	81 +77 = 158	23 +92 = 115

92 + 13 = __105__   73 + 83 = __156__

The Blues scored 63 points. The Reds scored 44 points. How many points were scored in all? __107__ points

9

10 — Subtraction: Regrouping

Subtraction means "taking away" or subtracting one number from another to find the difference. To regroup is to use one ten to form 10 ones, one hundred to form 10 tens, and so on.

Example:

32 = 2 tens + 12 ones
-13 = 1 ten + 3 ones
19 = 1 ten + 9 ones

Directions: Subtract using regrouping.

33 -28 = 5	86 -59 = 27	92 -37 = 55	71 -48 = 23

63 -47 = 16	45 -18 = 27	31 -22 = 9	55 -39 = 16

82 - 69 = __13__   73 - 36 = __37__

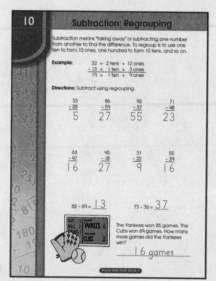

The Yankees won 85 games. The Cubs won 69 games. How many more games did the Yankees win? __16__ games

10

11 — Addition and Subtraction: Regrouping

Directions: Add or subtract. Regroup when needed.

92 -47 = 45	58 +26 = 84	63 +18 = 81	77 -38 = 39

27 -17 = 10	31 +42 = 73	56 -29 = 27	67 +33 = 100

72 +19 = 91	87 -58 = 29	93 -89 = 4	54 +27 = 81

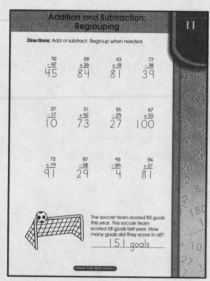

The soccer team scored 83 goals this year. The soccer team scored 68 goals last year. How many goals did they score in all? __151__ goals

11

12 — Review

Directions: Write this number on the blank:

four hundred thousands
five ten thousands
one thousand
eight hundreds
three tens
three ones

__4 5 1, 8 3 3__

Directions: Add or subtract. Use regrouping when needed.

87 -18 = 69	45 +29 = 74	95 -27 = 68	32 +19 = 51

86 -59 = 27	66 -39 = 27	74 +23 = 97	92 -67 = 25

57 + 18 = __75__   42 - 33 = __9__   35 + 19 = __54__

Sue won 75 tennis games. Jim won 59 tennis games. How many more games did Sue win? __16__ games

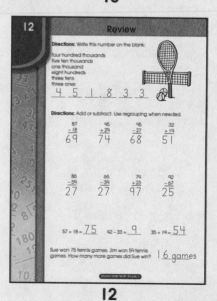

12

13 — Addition: Regrouping

Directions: Study the example. Add using regrouping.

Example:

Add the ones. Regroup.	Add the tens. Regroup.	Add the hundreds.
156 +267 = 3	6+7 = 13	156 +267 = 23	1+5+6 = 12	156 +267 = 423

273 +198 = 471	655 +297 = 952	783 +148 = 931	385 +169 = 554

29 46 +12 = 87	81 78 +33 = 192	52 67 +23 = 142	48 37 +19 = 105

Sally went bowling. She had scores of 105, 129, and 113. What was her total score for three games? __347__

13

Master Skills Math Grade 3

Answer Key

14 — Addition: Regrouping

Directions: Add using regrouping. Then, use the code to discover the name of a United States president. The first one is done for you.

348 + 752	642 + 277	386 + 787	184 + 875	578 + 874
1,100	919	1,173	1,059	1,452

653 + 768	653 + 359	946 + 239	393 + 257	199 + 843
1,421	1,012	1,185	650	1,042

721 + 679
1,400

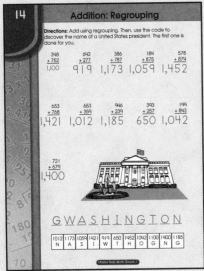

G W A S H I N G T O N

1012	1173	1059	1421	919	650	1452	1042	1100	1400	1185
N	A	S	I	W	T	H	O	G	N	G

Master Skills Math Grade 3

14

15 — Addition: Regrouping

Directions: Study the example. Add using regrouping.

Example:

5,356 + 3,976 = 9,332

Steps:
1. Add the ones.
2. Regroup the tens. Add the tens.
3. Regroup the hundreds. Add the hundreds.
4. Add the thousands.

6,849 + 3,276	1,846 + 8,384	9,221 + 6,769
10,125	10,230	15,990

2,758 + 3,663	5,299 + 8,764	7,932 + 6,879
6,421	14,063	14,811

A plane flew 1,838 miles on the first day. It flew 2,347 miles on the second day. How many miles did it fly in all?   **4,185 miles**

Master Skills Math Grade 3

15

16 — Addition: Mental Math

Directions: Try to do these addition problems in your head.

7 + 4	6 + 3	8 + 1	10 + 2	2 + 9
11	9	9	12	11

10 + 20	40 + 20	80 + 100	60 + 30	50 + 70
30	60	180	90	120

350 + 150	300 + 500	400 + 800	450 + 10	680 + 100
500	800	1,200	460	780

1,000 + 200	4,000 400 + 30	300 200 + 80	8,000 500 + 60	9,800 + 150
1,200	4,430	580	8,560	9,950

Master Skills Math Grade 3

16

17 — Subtraction: Regrouping

Directions: Regrouping for subtraction is the opposite of regrouping for addition. Study the example. Subtract using regrouping. Then, use the code to color the flowers.

Example:

647 − 453 = 194

Steps:
1. Subtract the ones.
2. Subtract the tens. Five tens cannot be subtracted from four tens.
3. Regroup the tens by regrouping six hundreds (five hundreds + 10 tens).
4. Add the 10 tens to the four tens.
5. Subtract five tens from 14 tens.
6. Subtract the hundreds.

If the answer has:
one one, color it red;
eight ones, color it pink;
five ones, color it yellow.

Master Skills Math Grade 3

17

18 — Subtraction: Regrouping

Directions: Study the example. Follow the steps. Subtract using regrouping.

Example:

634 − 455 = 179

Steps:
1. Subtract the ones. You cannot subtract five ones from four ones.
2. Regroup the ones by regrouping three tens to two tens + 10 ones.
3. Subtract five ones from 14 ones.
4. Regroup the tens by regrouping the hundreds (five hundreds + 10 tens).
5. Subtract five tens from 12 tens.
6. Subtract the hundreds.

635 − 169	553 − 174	832 − 563	944 − 578
466	379	269	366

423 − 268	941 − 872	733 − 498	266 − 197
155	69	235	69

387 − 198	594 − 384	960 − 759	887 − 598
189	210	201	289

Sophie goes to school 185 days a year. Yoko goes to school 313 days a year. How many more days of school does Yoko attend each year?   **128 days**

Master Skills Math Grade 3

18

19 — Subtraction: Regrouping

Directions: Study the example. Follow the steps. Subtract using regrouping. If you have to regroup to subtract ones and there are no tens, you must regroup twice.

Example:

300 − 182 = 118

Steps:
1. Subtract the ones. You cannot subtract two ones from zero ones.
2. Regroup. No tens. Regroup the hundreds (two hundreds + 10 tens).
3. Regroup the tens (nine tens + 10 ones).
4. Subtract two ones from 10 ones.
5. Subtract eight tens from nine tens.
6. Subtract one hundred from two hundreds.

602 − 423	306 − 128	600 − 263	807 − 499
179	178	337	308

800 − 557	206 − 137	400 − 224	508 − 379
243	69	176	129

207 − 138	604 − 397	308 − 199	700 − 531
69	207	109	169

Master Skills Math Grade 3

19

Answer Key

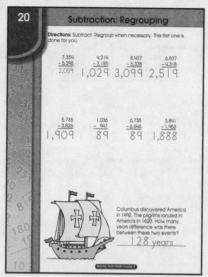

20 — Subtraction: Regrouping

Directions: Subtract. Regroup when necessary. The first one is done for you.

7,354 − 5,295	4,214 − 3,185	8,437 − 5,338	6,837 − 4,318
2,059	1,029	3,099	2,519

5,735 − 3,826	1,036 − 947	6,735 − 6,646	3,841 − 1,953
1,909	89	89	1,888

Columbus discovered America in 1492. The pilgrims landed in America in 1620. How many years difference was there between these two events?

128 years

20

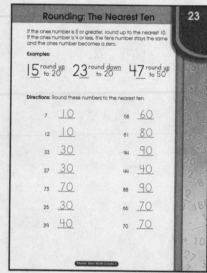

21 — Subtraction: Mental Math

Directions: Try to do these subtraction problems in your head.

9 − 3	12 − 6	7 − 6	5 − 1	15 − 5
6	6	1	4	10

40 − 20	90 − 80	100 − 50	20 − 20	60 − 10
20	10	50	0	50

450 − 250	500 − 300	250 − 20	690 − 100	320 − 20
200	200	230	590	300

1,000 − 400	8,000 − 500	7,000 − 900	4,000 − 2,000	9,500 − 4,000
600	7,500	6,100	2,000	5,500

21

22 — Review

Directions: Add or subtract using regrouping.

28 56 + 93	82 49 + 51	33 75 + 128	67 94 + 248
177	182	236	409

683 − 495	756 + 139	818 − 387	956 + 267
188	895	431	1,223

1,588 − 989	4,675 − 2,976	8,732 − 5,664	2,938 + 3,459
599	1,699	3,068	6,397

The drive from New York City to Los Angeles is 2,832 miles. The drive from New York City to Miami is 1,327 miles. How much farther is it to drive from New York City to Los Angeles than from New York City to Miami?

1,505 miles

22

23 — Rounding: The Nearest Ten

If the ones number is 5 or greater, round up to the nearest 10. If the ones number is 4 or less, the tens number stays the same and the ones number becomes a zero.

Examples:

15 round up to 20   23 round down to 20   47 round up to 50

Directions: Round these numbers to the nearest ten.

7	10	58	60
12	10	81	80
33	30	94	90
27	30	44	40
73	70	88	90
25	30	66	70
39	40	70	70

23

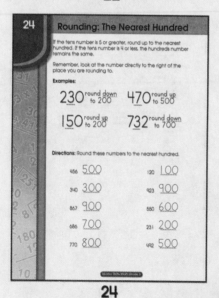

24 — Rounding: The Nearest Hundred

If the tens number is 5 or greater, round up to the nearest hundred. If the tens number is 4 or less, the hundreds number remains the same.

Remember, look at the number directly to the right of the place you are rounding to.

Examples:

230 round down to 200   470 round up to 500

150 round up to 200   732 round down to 700

Directions: Round these numbers to the nearest hundred.

456	500	120	100
340	300	923	900
867	900	550	600
686	700	231	200
770	800	492	500

24

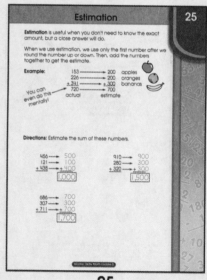

25 — Estimation

Estimation is useful when you don't need to know the exact amount, but a close answer will do.

When we use estimation, we use only the first number after we round the number up or down. Then, add the numbers together to get the estimate.

Example:

153	→	200	apples
226	→	200	oranges
+ 341	→	+ 300	bananas
720		700	
actual		estimate	

You can even do this mentally!

Directions: Estimate the sum of these numbers.

456	→	500	910	→	900
121	→	100	280	→	300
+ 438	→	+ 400	+ 320	→	+ 300
		1,000			1,500

686	→	700
307	→	300
+ 711	→	+ 700
		1,700

25

26 — Multiplication

Multiplication is a short way to find the sum of adding the same number a certain amount of times. For example, we write 7 x 4 = 28 instead of 7 + 7 + 7 + 7 = 28.

Directions: Study the example. Multiply.

Example:

There are two groups of seashells.
There are three seashells in each group.
How many seashells are there in all?

2 x 3 = 6

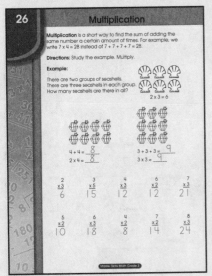

4 + 4 = __8__
2 x 4 = __8__

3 + 3 + 3 = __9__
3 x 3 = __9__

2 x3	3 x5	4 x3	6 x2	7 x3
6	15	12	12	21

5 x2	6 x3	4 x2	7 x2	8 x3
10	18	8	14	24

26

27 — Multiplication

Directions: Multiply.

3 x5	4 x6	3 x8
15	24	24

5 x5	4 x8	5 x4
25	32	20

6 x7	3 x9	8 x2	7 x6	9 x4
42	27	16	42	36

6 x8	5 x6	7 x7	5 x3	8 x9
48	30	49	15	72

A river boat makes three trips a day every day. How many trips does it make in a week? __21 trips__

27

28 — Multiplication

Factors are the numbers multiplied together in a multiplication problem. The answer is called the **product**. If you change the order of the factors, the product stays the same.

Example:

There are four groups of fish.
There are three fish in each group.
How many fish are there in all?

4 x 3 = 12
factor x factor = product

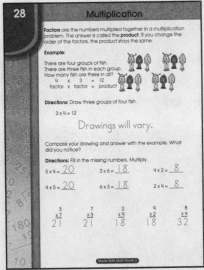

Directions: Draw three groups of four fish.

3 x 4 = 12

Drawings will vary.

Compare your drawing and answer with the example. What did you notice?

Directions: Fill in the missing numbers. Multiply.

5 x 4 = __20__   3 x 6 = __18__   4 x 2 = __8__

4 x 5 = __20__   6 x 3 = __18__   2 x 4 = __8__

3 x7	7 x3	2 x9	9 x2	8 x4
21	21	18	18	32

28

29 — Multiplication: Zero And One

Any number multiplied by zero equals zero. One multiplied by any number equals that number.

Example:

How many full sails are there in all?

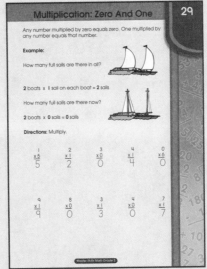

2 boats x **1** sail on each boat = **2** sails

How many full sails are there now?

2 boats x **0** sails = **0** sails

Directions: Multiply.

1 x5	2 x1	3 x0	4 x1	0 x6
5	2	0	4	0

9 x1	8 x0	3 x1	4 x0	7 x1
9	0	3	0	7

29

30 — Multiplication

Directions: Time yourself as you multiply. How quickly can you complete this page?

3 x2	8 x7	1 x0	1 x6	3 x4
6	56	0	6	12

1 x4	4 x4	2 x5	3 x9	9 x9
4	16	10	27	81

0 x8	2 x6	9 x6	8 x5	7 x3
0	12	54	40	21

3 x5	2 x0	4 x6	1 x3	0 x0
15	0	24	3	0

30

31 — Multiplication Table

Directions: Complete the multiplication table. Use it to practice your multiplication facts.

x	0	1	2	3	4	5	6	7	8	9	10
0	0	0	0	0	0	0	0	0	0	0	0
1	0	1	2	3	4	5	6	7	8	9	10
2	0	2	4	6	8	10	12	14	16	18	20
3	0	3	6	9	12	15	18	21	24	27	30
4	0	4	8	12	16	20	24	28	32	36	40
5	0	5	10	15	20	25	30	35	40	45	50
6	0	6	12	18	24	30	36	42	48	54	60
7	0	7	14	21	28	35	42	49	56	63	70
8	0	8	16	24	32	40	48	56	64	72	80
9	0	9	18	27	36	45	54	63	72	81	90
10	0	10	20	30	40	50	60	70	80	90	100

31

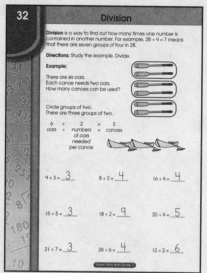

32 — Division

Division is a way to find out how many times one number is contained in another number. For example, 28 ÷ 4 = 7 means that there are seven groups of four in 28.

Directions: Study the example. Divide.

Example:

There are six oars.
Each canoe needs two oars.
How many canoes can be used?

Circle groups of two.
There are three groups of two.

6 + 2 = 3
oars + numbers = canoes
of oars
needed
per canoe

9 ÷ 3 = 3   8 ÷ 2 = 4   16 ÷ 4 = 4

15 ÷ 5 = 3   18 ÷ 2 = 9   20 ÷ 4 = 5

21 ÷ 7 = 3   24 ÷ 6 = 4   12 ÷ 2 = 6

32

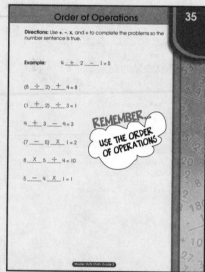

33 — Division

Directions: Divide. Draw a line from the boat to the sail with the correct answer. The first one is done for you.

42 ÷ 6 → 7
32 ÷ 8 → 4
24 ÷ 4 → 6
35 ÷ 7 → 5
27 ÷ 9 → 3
18 ÷ 9 → 2

33

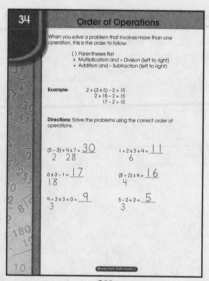

34 — Order of Operations

When you solve a problem that involves more than one operation, this is the order to follow:

( ) Parentheses first
x Multiplication and ÷ Division (left to right)
+ Addition and − Subtraction (left to right)

Example: 2 + (3 x 5) − 2 = 15
                       2 + 15 − 2 = 15
                           17 − 2 = 15

Directions: Solve the problems using the correct order of operations.

(5 − 3) + 4 x 7 = 30   1 + 2 x 3 + 4 = 11
2   28   6

6 x 3 − 1 = 17   (8 ÷ 2) x 4 = 16
18   4

9 ÷ 3 x 3 + 0 = 9   5 − 2 + 2 = 5
3   3

34

35 — Order of Operations

Directions: Use +, −, x, and ÷ to complete the problems so the number sentence is true.

Example: 4 + 2 − 1 = 5

(8 ÷ 2) + 4 = 8

(1 + 2) ÷ 3 = 1

9 + 3 − 9 = 3

(7 − 5) x 1 = 2

8 x 5 ÷ 4 = 10

5 − 4 x 1 = 1

REMEMBER...
USE THE ORDER OF OPERATIONS

35

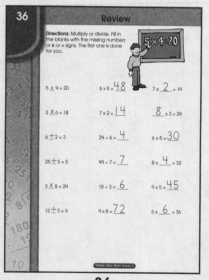

36 — Review

Directions: Multiply or divide. Fill in the blanks with the missing numbers or x or ÷ signs. The first one is done for you.

5 x 4 = 20   6 x 8 = 48   7 x 2 = 14

3 X 6 = 18   7 x 2 = 14   8 x 3 = 24

6 ÷ 2 = 3   24 ÷ 6 = 4   6 x 5 = 30

25 ÷ 5 = 5   49 ÷ 7 = 7   8 x 4 = 32

3 X 8 = 24   18 ÷ 3 = 6   9 x 5 = 45

12 ÷ 3 = 4   9 x 8 = 72   6 x 6 = 36

36

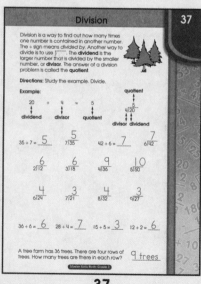

37 — Division

Division is a way to find out how many times one number is contained in another number. The ÷ sign means divided by. Another way to divide is to use ⟌. The **dividend** is the larger number that is divided by the smaller number, or **divisor**. The answer of a division problem is called the **quotient**.

Directions: Study the example. Divide.

Example:

20 ÷ 4 = 5
dividend divisor quotient

quotient
5
4⟌20
divisor dividend

35 ÷ 7 = 5   7⟌35   42 ÷ 6 = 7   6⟌42

6   6   9   10
2⟌12   3⟌18   4⟌36   5⟌50

4   3   4   3
6⟌24   7⟌21   8⟌32   9⟌27

36 ÷ 6 = 6   28 ÷ 4 = 7   15 ÷ 5 = 3   12 ÷ 2 = 6

A tree farm has 36 trees. There are four rows of trees. How many trees are there in each row?   9 trees

37

38 — Division: Zero and One

Directions: Study the rules of division and the examples. Divide, then write the number of the rule you used to solve each problem.

Examples:

Rule 1: $1)\overline{5}$ (5) Any number divided by 1 is that number.

Rule 2: $5)\overline{5}$ (1) Any number except 0 divided by itself is 1.

Rule 3: $7)\overline{0}$ (0) Zero divided by any number is zero.

Rule 4: $0)\overline{17}$ You cannot divide by zero.

$1)\overline{6}$ **6** Rule **1** $1)\overline{7}$ **7** Rule **1**

ZERO ONE

$7)\overline{7}$ Rule **2** $0)\overline{15}$ Rule **4**

$9)\overline{0}$ **0** Rule **3** $1)\overline{4}$ **4** Rule **1**

39 — Division: Remainders

Division is a way to find out how many times one number is contained in another number. For example, 28 ÷ 7 = 7 means that there are seven groups of four in 28. The **dividend** is the larger number that is divided by the smaller number, or **divisor**. The **quotient** is the answer in a division problem. The **remainder** is the amount left over. The remainder is always less than the divisor.

Directions: Study the example. Find each quotient and remainder.

Example:
There are 11 dog biscuits.
Put them in groups of three.
There are two left over.

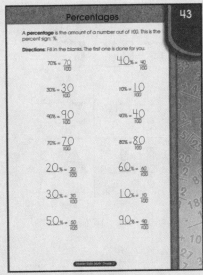

$3)\overline{11}$ (3) $3)\overline{11}$ (3 r2)   **Remember:** The remainder must
-9 be less than the divisor!
$\overline{2}$ remainder

$3)\overline{13}$ **4 r1** $4)\overline{17}$ **4 r1** $6)\overline{32}$ **5 r2** $5)\overline{26}$ **5 r1**

$9 ÷ 4 = $ **2 r 1** $12 ÷ 5 = $ **2 r 2** $26 ÷ 4 = $ **6 r 2** $49 ÷ 9 = $ **5 r 4**

The pet store has seven cats. Two cats go in each cage. How many cats are left over? ___**1 cat**___

40 — Multiples

Directions: Draw a red circle around the numbers that can be divided by 2. We say these are multiples of two. Draw a blue **X** on the multiples of three. Draw a green square around the multiples of five. Draw a yellow circle around the multiples of ten.

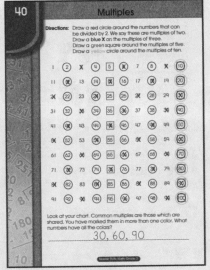

Look at your chart. Common multiples are those which are shared. You have marked them in more than one color. What numbers have all the colors?
___**30, 60, 90**___

41 — Divisibility Rules

A number is divisible...
  by 2 if the last digit is 0 or even (2, 4, 6, 8).
  by 3 if the sum of all digits is divisible by 3.
  by 4 if the last two digits are divisible by 4.
  by 5 if the last digit is a 0 or 5.
  by 10 if the last digit is 0.

Example: 250 is divisible by **2, 5, 10**

Directions: Look at the numbers below. Tell if the number is divisible by 2, 3, 4, 5, or 10 using the key above.

3,732 **2, 3, 4**   439 ___—___

50 **2, 5, 10**   444 **2, 3, 4**

7,960 **2, 4, 5, 10**   8,212 **2, 4**

104,924 **2, 4**   2,345 **5**

42 — Factor Trees

Factors are the smaller numbers multiplied together to make a larger number. Factor trees are one way to find all the factors of a number.

Example:

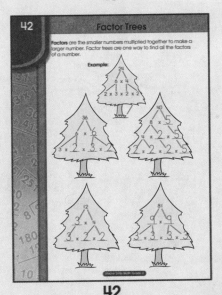

43 — Percentages

A **percentage** is the amount of a number out of 100. This is the percent sign: %.

Directions: Fill in the blanks. The first one is done for you.

$70\% = \dfrac{70}{100}$ $40\% = \dfrac{40}{100}$

$30\% = \dfrac{30}{100}$ $10\% = \dfrac{10}{100}$

$90\% = \dfrac{90}{100}$ $40\% = \dfrac{40}{100}$

$70\% = \dfrac{70}{100}$ $80\% = \dfrac{80}{100}$

$20\% = \dfrac{20}{100}$ $60\% = \dfrac{60}{100}$

$30\% = \dfrac{30}{100}$ $10\% = \dfrac{10}{100}$

$50\% = \dfrac{50}{100}$ $90\% = \dfrac{90}{100}$

Answer Key

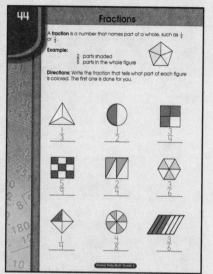

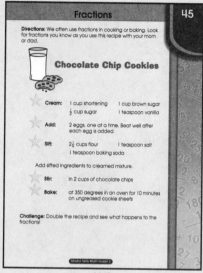

44

45

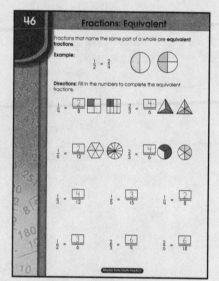

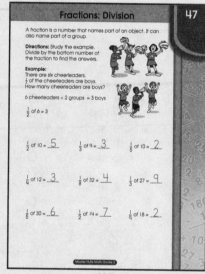

46

47

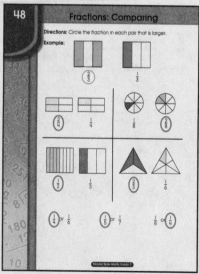

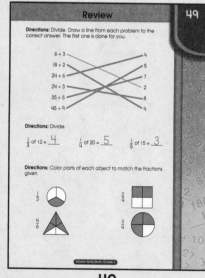

48

49

Master Skills Math Grade 3

Answer Key

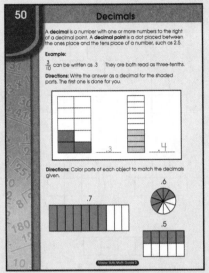

50

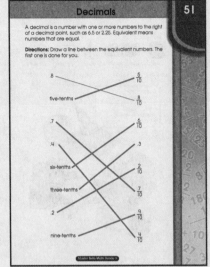

51

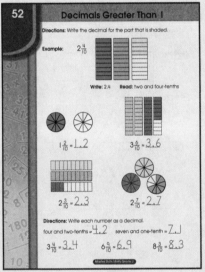

52

53

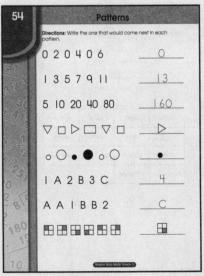

54

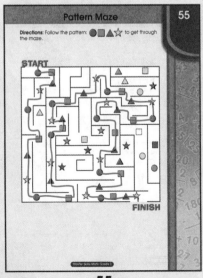

55

56 Geometry

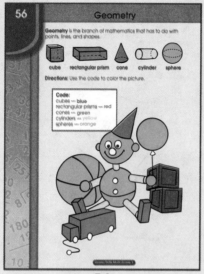

56

57 Geometry

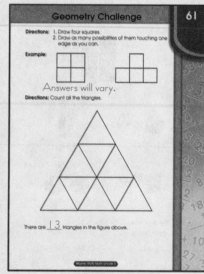

57

59 Tangram

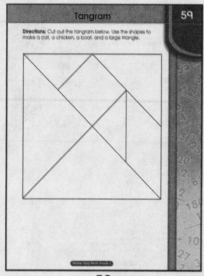

59

61 Geometry Challenge

Directions: 1. Draw four squares.
2. Draw as many possibilities of them touching one edge as you can.

Example:

Answers will vary.

Directions: Count all the triangles.

There are 13 triangles in the figure above.

61

62 Geometry: Lines, Segments, Rays, Angles

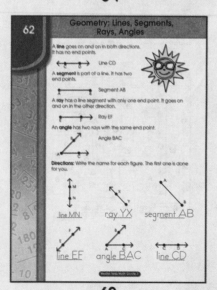

62

63 Geometry Game

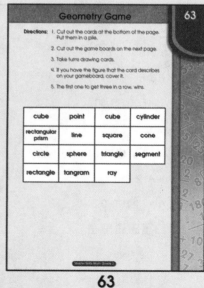

63

65 — Geometry Game

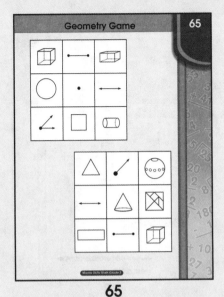

65

67 — Geometry: Perimeter

The **perimeter** is the distance around an object. Find the perimeter by adding the lengths of all the sides.

Directions: Find the perimeter for each object (ft. = feet). The first one is done for you.

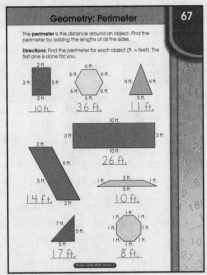

67

68 — Geometric Coloring

Directions: Color the geometric shapes in the box below.

Colors will vary.

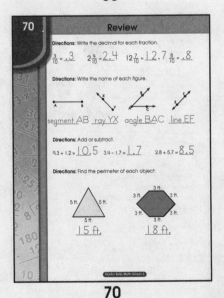

68

69 — Flower Power

Directions: Count the flowers and answer the questions.

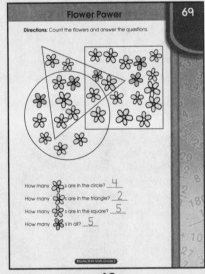

How many flowers are in the circle? __4__

How many flowers are in the triangle? __2__

How many flowers are in the square? __5__

How many flowers in all? __5__

69

70 — Review

Directions: Write the decimal for each fraction.

$\frac{3}{10}$ = .3 $2\frac{4}{10}$ = 2.4 $12\frac{7}{10}$ = 12.7 $\frac{8}{10}$ = .8

Directions: Write the name of each figure.

segment AB   ray YX   angle BAC   line EF

Directions: Add or subtract.

9.3 + 1.2 = 10.5   3.4 − 1.7 = 1.7   2.8 + 5.7 = 8.5

Directions: Find the perimeter of each object.

15 ft.   18 ft.

70

71 — Graphs

A **graph** is a drawing that shows information about numbers.

Directions: Color the picture. Then, tell how many there are of each object by completing the graph.

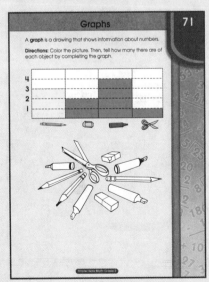

71

Answer Key

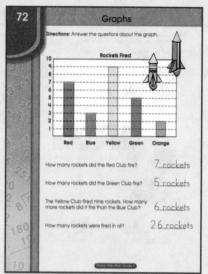

72 — Graphs

Directions: Answer the questions about the graph.

Rockets Fired

How many rockets did the Red Club fire? 7 rockets

How many rockets did the Green Club fire? 5 rockets

The Yellow Club fired nine rockets. How many more rockets did it fire than the Blue Club? 6 rockets

How many rockets were fired in all? 26 rockets

72

73 — Measurement: Inches

An **inch** is a unit of length in the standard measurement system.

Directions: Use a ruler to measure each object to the nearest $\frac{1}{4}$ inch. Write **in.** to stand for inch.

Examples: 1 in. 2½ in.

2½ in.   2½ in.

2¼ in.   1¼ in.

4 in.

73

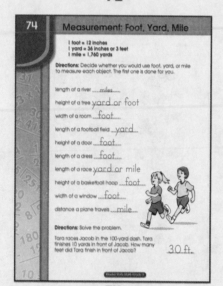

74 — Measurement: Foot, Yard, Mile

1 foot = 12 inches
1 yard = 36 inches or 3 feet
1 mile = 1,760 yards

Directions: Decide whether you would use foot, yard, or mile to measure each object. The first one is done for you.

length of a river — miles

height of a tree — yard or foot

width of a room — foot

length of a football field — yard

height of a door — foot

length of a dress — foot

length of a race — yard or mile

height of a basketball hoop — foot

width of a window — foot

distance a plane travels — mile

Directions: Solve the problem.

Tara races Jacob in the 100-yard dash. Tara finishes 10 yards in front of Jacob. How many feet did Tara finish in front of Jacob? 30 ft.

74

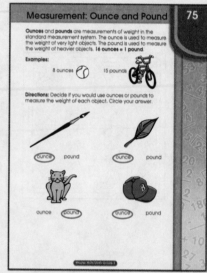

75 — Measurement: Ounce and Pound

Ounces and **pounds** are measurements of weight in the standard measurement system. The ounce is used to measure the weight of very light objects. The pound is used to measure the weight of heavier objects. **16 ounces = 1 pound.**

Examples: 8 ounces   15 pounds

Directions: Decide if you would use ounces or pounds to measure the weight of each object. Circle your answer.

(ounce) pound   (ounce) pound

ounce (pound)   (ounce) pound

75

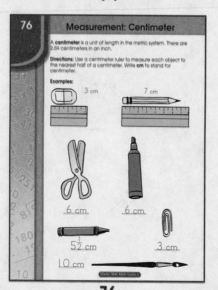

76 — Measurement: Centimeter

A **centimeter** is a unit of length in the metric system. There are 2.54 centimeters in an inch.

Directions: Use a centimeter ruler to measure each object to the nearest half of a centimeter. Write **cm** to stand for centimeter.

Examples: 3 cm   7 cm

6 cm   6 cm

5½ cm   3 cm

10 cm

76

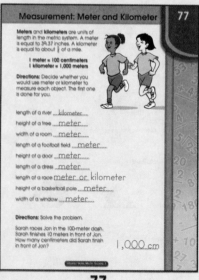

77 — Measurement: Meter and Kilometer

Meters and **kilometers** are units of length in the metric system. A meter is equal to 39.37 inches. A kilometer is equal to about $\frac{2}{3}$ of a mile.

1 meter = 100 centimeters
1 kilometer = 1,000 meters

Directions: Decide whether you would use meter or kilometer to measure each object. The first one is done for you.

length of a river — kilometer

height of a tree — meter

width of a room — meter

length of a football field — meter

height of a door — meter

length of a dress — meter

length of a race — meter or kilometer

height of a basketball pole — meter

width of a window — meter

Directions: Solve the problem.

Sarah races Jon in the 100-meter dash. Sarah finishes 10 meters in front of Jon. How many centimeters did Sarah finish in front of Jon? 1,000 cm

77

Answer Key

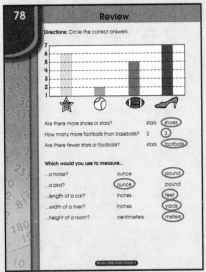

78 — Review

Directions: Circle the correct answers.

Are there more shoes or stars? stars **(shoes)**

How many more footballs than baseballs? 2 **(3)**

Are there fewer stars or footballs? **(stars)** footballs

Which would you use to measure...

...a horse? ounce **(pound)**

...a bird? **(ounce)** pound

...length of a car? inches **(feet)**

...width of a river? inches **(yards)**

...height of a room? centimeters **(meters)**

78

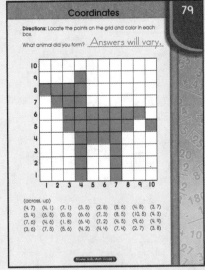

79 — Coordinates

Directions: Locate the points on the grid and color in each box.

What animal did you form? __Answers will vary.__

(across, up)

(4, 7) (4, 1) (7, 1) (3, 5) (2, 8) (8, 6) (4, 8) (3, 7)
(5, 4) (5, 5) (6, 5) (6, 6) (7, 3) (8, 5) (10, 5) (4, 3)
(7, 6) (4, 6) (1, 8) (6, 4) (7, 2) (4, 5) (9, 6) (4, 9)
(3, 6) (7, 5) (5, 6) (4, 2) (4, 4) (7, 4) (2, 7) (3, 8)

79

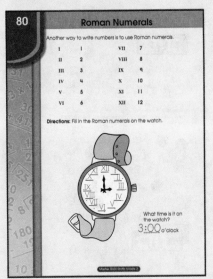

80 — Roman Numerals

Another way to write numbers is to use Roman numerals.

I	1	VII	7
II	2	VIII	8
III	3	IX	9
IV	4	X	10
V	5	XI	11
VI	6	XII	12

Directions: Fill in the Roman numerals on the watch.

What time is it on the watch? **3:00** o'clock

80

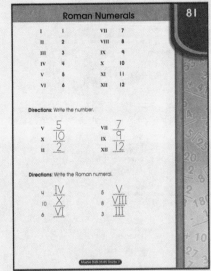

81 — Roman Numerals

I	1	VII	7
II	2	VIII	8
III	3	IX	9
IV	4	X	10
V	5	XI	11
VI	6	XII	12

Directions: Write the number.

V **5**   VII **7**
X **10**   IX **9**
II **2**   XII **12**

Directions: Write the Roman numeral.

4 **IV**   5 **V**
10 **X**   8 **VIII**
6 **VI**   3 **III**

81

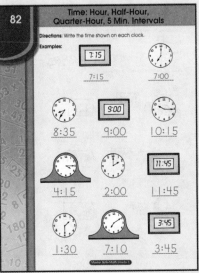

82 — Time: Hour, Half-Hour, Quarter-Hour, 5 Min. Intervals

Directions: Write the time shown on each clock.

Examples:

7:15   7:00

8:35   9:00   10:15

4:15   2:00   11:45

1:30   7:10   3:45

82

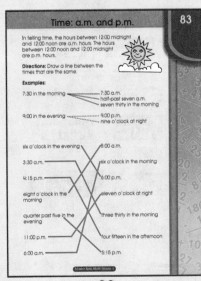

83 — Time: a.m. and p.m.

In telling time, the hours between 12:00 midnight and 12:00 noon are a.m. hours. The hours between 12:00 noon and 12:00 midnight are p.m. hours.

Directions: Draw a line between the times that are the same.

Examples:

7:30 in the morning — 7:30 a.m. / half-past seven a.m. / seven thirty in the morning

9:00 in the evening — 9:00 p.m. / nine o'clock at night

six o'clock in the evening — 6:00 a.m.

3:30 a.m. — six o'clock in the morning

4:15 p.m. — 6:00 p.m.

eight o'clock in the morning — eleven o'clock at night

quarter past five in the evening — three thirty in the morning

11:00 p.m. — four fifteen in the afternoon

6:00 a.m. — 5:15 p.m.

83

Master Skills Math Grade 3

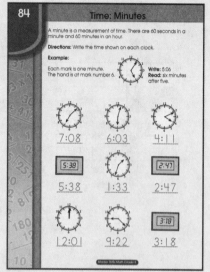

84 — Time: Minutes

A minute is a measurement of time. There are 60 seconds in a minute and 60 minutes in an hour.

Directions: Write the time shown on each clock.

Example:
Each mark is one minute. The hand is at mark number 6.
Write: 5:06
Read: six minutes after five.

7:08 6:03 4:11
5:38 1:33 2:47
12:01 9:22 3:18

84

---

85 — Time: Addition

Directions: Add the hours and minutes together.
(Remember, 1 hour equals 60 minutes.)

Examples:
2 hours 10 minutes
+ 1 hour 50 minutes
3 hours 60 minutes
(1 hour)
4 hours

4 hours 20 minutes
+ 2 hours 10 minutes
6 hours 30 minutes

9 hours
+ 2 hours
11 hours

1 hour
+ 5 hours
6 hours

6 hours
+ 3 hours
9 hours

6 hours 15 minutes
+ 1 hour 15 minutes
7 hours 30 minutes

10 hours 30 minutes
+ 1 hour 10 minutes
11 hours 40 minutes

3 hours 40 minutes
+ 8 hours 20 minutes
12 hours

11 hours 15 minutes
+ 1 hour 30 minutes
12 hours 45 minutes

4 hours 15 minutes
+ 5 hours 45 minutes
10 hours

7 hours 10 minutes
+ 1 hour 30 minutes
8 hours 40 minutes

85

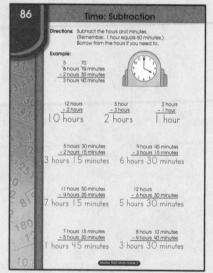

86 — Time: Subtraction

Directions: Subtract the hours and minutes.
(Remember, 1 hour equals 60 minutes.)
Borrow from the hours if you need to.

Example:
5 70
6 hours 10 minutes
– 2 hours 30 minutes
3 hours 40 minutes

12 hours
– 2 hours
10 hours

5 hour
– 3 hours
2 hours

2 hours
– 1 hour
1 hour

5 hours 30 minutes
– 2 hours 15 minutes
3 hours 15 minutes

9 hours 45 minutes
– 3 hours 15 minutes
6 hours 30 minutes

11 hours 50 minutes
– 4 hours 35 minutes
7 hours 15 minutes

12 hours
– 6 hours 30 minutes
5 hours 30 minutes

7 hours 15 minutes
– 5 hours 30 minutes
1 hours 45 minutes

8 hours 10 minutes
– 4 hours 40 minutes
3 hours 30 minutes

86

---

87 — Money: Coins and Dollars

dollar = 100¢ or $1.00
penny = 1¢ or $.01
nickel = 5¢ or $.05
dime = 10¢ or $.10
quarter = 25¢ or $.25
half-dollar = 50¢ or $.50

Directions: Write the amount for each group of money shown. Use a dollar sign and decimal point. The first one is done for you.

$0.07 or 7¢ $.11 or 7¢
$.36 or 36¢ $.32 or 32¢
$2.55

87

88 — Money: Five-Dollar Bill and Ten-Dollar Bill

Five-dollar bill = 5 one-dollar bills
Ten-dollar bill = 2 five-dollar bills or 10 one-dollar bills

Directions: Write the amount for each group of money shown. Use a dollar sign and decimal point. The first one is done for you.

$15.00 $6.35
$6.00 $16.31

7 one-dollar bills, 2 quarters $7.50
2 five-dollar bills, 3 one-dollar bills, half-dollar $13.50

88

89 — Money: Counting Change

Directions: Subtract the money using decimals to show how much change a person would receive in each of the following.

Example:
Bill had 3 dollars.
He bought a baseball for $2.83.
How much change did he receive?
$3.00
– $2.83
$ .17

$2.83

Paid 2 dollars. $1.75
$.25 or 25¢

Paid 1 dollar. 83¢
$.17 or 17¢

Paid 5 dollars. $4.35
$.65 or 65¢

$8.55
$1.45

Paid 10 dollars.

Paid 4 dollars. $3.98
$.02 or 2¢

Paid 7 dollars. $6.38
$.62 or 62¢

89

Answer Key

90 — Money: Comparing

Directions: Compare the amount of money in the left column with the price of the object in the right column. Is the amount of money in the left column enough to purchase the object in the right column? Circle **yes** or **no**.

- $1.75 — (Yes) No
- $6.95 — Yes (No)
- $.55 — (Yes) No
- $12.85 — (Yes) No

90

91 — Review

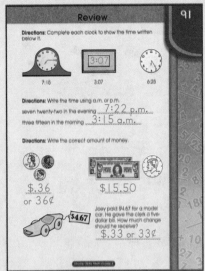

Directions: Complete each clock to show the time written below it.

7:18   3:07   6:28

Directions: Write the time using a.m. or p.m.

seven twenty-two in the evening — 7:22 p.m.
three fifteen in the morning — 3:15 a.m.

Directions: Write the correct amount of money.

$.36 or 36¢ $15.50

Joey paid $4.67 for a model car. He gave the clerk a five-dollar bill. How much change should he receive?
$.33 or 33¢

91

92 — Problem-Solving: Addition, Subtraction

Directions: Read and solve each problem. The first one is done for you.

The clown started the day with 200 balloons. He gave away 128 of them. Some broke. At the end of the day, he had 18 balloons left. How many of the balloons broke? — 54 balloons

On Monday, there were 925 tickets sold to adults and 1,412 tickets sold to children. How many more children attended the fair than adults? — 487 more children

At one game booth, prizes were given out for scoring 500 points in three attempts. Sydney scored 178 points on her first attempt, 149 points on her second attempt, and 233 points on her third attempt. Did Sydney win a prize? — yes

The prize-winning steer weighed 2,348 pounds. The runner-up steer weighed 2,179 pounds. How much more did the prize steer weigh? — 169 pounds

92

93 — Problem-Solving: Multiplication, Division

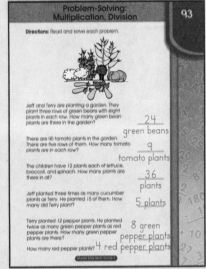

Directions: Read and solve each problem.

Jeff and Terry are planting a garden. They plant three rows of green beans with eight plants in each row. How many green bean plants are there in the garden? — 24 green beans

There are 45 tomato plants in the garden. There are five rows of them. How many tomato plants are in each row? — 9 tomato plants

The children have 12 plants each of lettuce, broccoli, and spinach. How many plants are there in all? — 36 plants

Jeff planted three times as many cucumber plants as Terry. He planted 15 of them. How many did Terry plant? — 5 plants

Terry planted 12 pepper plants. He planted twice as many green pepper plants as red pepper plants. How many green pepper plants are there? — 8 green pepper plants
How many red pepper plants? — 4 red pepper plants

93

94 — Problem-Solving: Fractions, Decimals

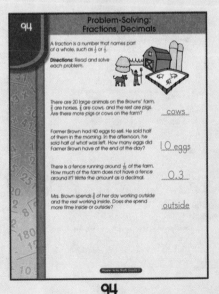

A fraction is a number that names part of a whole, such as $\frac{1}{2}$ or $\frac{1}{3}$.

Directions: Read and solve each problem.

There are 20 large animals on the Browns' farm. $\frac{2}{5}$ are horses, $\frac{1}{4}$ are cows, and the rest are pigs. Are there more pigs or cows on the farm? — cows

Farmer Brown had 40 eggs to sell. He sold half of them in the morning. In the afternoon, he sold half of what was left. How many eggs did Farmer Brown have at the end of the day? — 10 eggs

There is a fence running around $\frac{7}{10}$ of the farm. How much of the farm does not have a fence around it? Write the amount as a decimal. — 0.3

Mrs. Brown spends $\frac{2}{5}$ of her day working outside and the rest working inside. Does she spend more time inside or outside? — outside

94

95 — Problem-Solving: Measurement

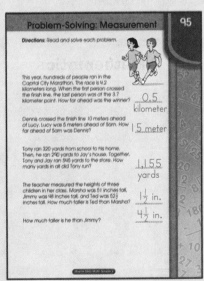

Directions: Read and solve each problem.

This year, hundreds of people ran in the Capital City Marathon. The race is 4.2 kilometers long. When the first person crossed the finish line, the last person was at the 3.7 kilometer point. How far ahead was the winner? — 0.5 kilometer

Dennis crossed the finish line 10 meters ahead of Lucy. Lucy was 5 meters ahead of Sam. How far ahead of Sam was Dennis? — 15 meter

Tony ran 320 yards from school to his home. Then, he ran 290 yards to Jay's house. Together, Tony and Jay ran 545 yards to the store. How many yards in all did Tony run? — 1,155 yards

The teacher measured the heights of three children in her class. Marsha was 51 inches tall, Jimmy was 48 inches tall, and Ted was $52\frac{1}{2}$ inches tall. How much taller is Ted than Marsha? — $1\frac{1}{2}$ in.

How much taller is he than Jimmy? — $4\frac{1}{2}$ in.

95

Answer Key

---

96 Problem-Solving: Measurement

Directions: Read and solve each problem.

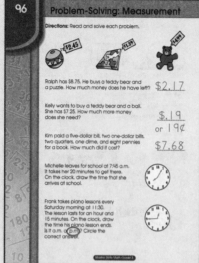

Ralph has $8.75. He buys a teddy bear and a puzzle. How much money does he have left? **$2.17**

Kelly wants to buy a teddy bear and a ball. She has $7.25. How much more money does she need? **$.19 or 19¢**

Kim paid a five-dollar bill, two one-dollar bills, two quarters, one dime, and eight pennies for a book. How much did it cost? **$7.68**

Michelle leaves for school at 7:45 a.m. It takes her 20 minutes to get there. On the clock, draw the time that she arrives at school.

Frank takes piano lessons every Saturday morning at 11:30. The lesson lasts for an hour and 15 minutes. On the clock, draw the time his piano lesson ends. Is it a.m. or p.m.? Circle the correct answer.

96

---

97 Review

Directions: Read and solve each of the problems.

The baker sets out nine baking pans with six rolls on each one. How many rolls are there in all? **54 rolls**

A dozen brownies cost $1.29. James pays for a dozen brownies with a five-dollar bill. How much change does he receive? **$3.71**

Theresa has four quarters, a nickel, and three pennies. How much more money does she need to buy brownies? **$.21 or 21¢**

The baker made 24 loaves of bread. At the end of the day, he has ¼ left. How many did he sell? **18 loaves**

The bakery opens at 8:30 a.m. It closes nine and a half hours later. What time does it close? **6:00 p.m.**

97

---

98 Math Terms Crossword

Directions: Use your glossary and the clues on page 99 to help you fill in the words.

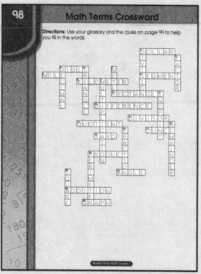

98

---

99 Math Terms Crossword

Across:
1. 100¢
3. Symbols used to write numbers
6. A measurement of distance in the standard measurement system that is equal to 1,760 yards
7. Part of a line with two end points
8. A measurement in the metric system of a great distance
10. A figure with four corners and four sides
12. Answer in a subtraction problem
13. Smaller number that is divided into the dividend
14. Answer of a division problem
17. A measurement of weight in the standard measurement system of a very light object
18. A measurement of distance in the standard measurement system that is equal to 36 inches
19. Answer in a multiplication problem
21. Two rays with the same end point
22. Putting together two or more numbers to find the sum

23. A drawing that shows information about numbers

Down:
1. Operation to find out how many times one number is contained in another
2. A number multiplied together in a problem
3. A number with one or more places to the right
4. A figure with three corners and three sides
5. A measurement of length in the metric system of a short distance
9. A short way to find the sum of adding the same number many times
11. A point at the end of a line segment or ray
15. The number left over in the quotient
16. A number that names part of a whole
19. Distance around an object
20. A figure with four corners and four sides of equal length

99

---

100 Challenge

Directions: See how many words you can make from the letters in the word **Mathematics**.

Mathematics
Answers will vary.

For a challenge, time yourself or race another person.

100

---

101 Review

Directions: Write the number's value in each place: **678,421**.

1 ones	**6** hundred thousands
8 thousands	**4** hundreds
2 tens	**7** ten thousands

Directions: Add or subtract. Remember to regroup, if you need to.

```
  88      46      75      93
- 19    + 39    + 24    - 68
  69      85      99      25
```

```
 683      84      97     9,731
-496     49      54    - 4,664
 187    + 62    + 361    5,067
         195     512
```

Directions: Round to the nearest ten, hundred, or thousand.

```
72  70    49  50    31  30    66  70
151 200   296 300   917 900   621 600
```

101

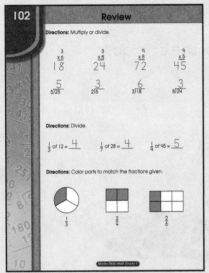

102

Review

Directions: Multiply or divide.

$$\begin{array}{c}3\\\times 6\\\hline 18\end{array} \qquad \begin{array}{c}3\\\times 8\\\hline 24\end{array} \qquad \begin{array}{c}9\\\times 8\\\hline 72\end{array} \qquad \begin{array}{c}9\\\times 5\\\hline 45\end{array}$$

$$5\overline{)25} \to 5 \qquad 2\overline{)6} \to 3 \qquad 3\overline{)18} \to 6 \qquad 8\overline{)24} \to 3$$

Directions: Divide.

$\frac{1}{3}$ of 12 = 4 $\frac{1}{7}$ of 28 = 4 $\frac{1}{9}$ of 45 = 5

Directions: Color parts to match the fractions given.

$\frac{1}{3}$ $\frac{2}{4}$ $\frac{2}{6}$

102

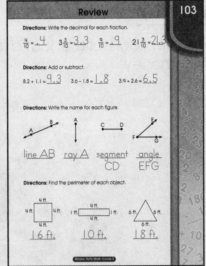

103

Review

Directions: Write the decimal for each fraction.

$\frac{4}{10}$ = .4 $3\frac{3}{10}$ = 3.3 $\frac{9}{10}$ = .9 $21\frac{3}{10}$ = 21.3

Directions: Add or subtract.

8.2 + 1.1 = 9.3   3.6 - 1.8 = 1.8   3.9 + 2.6 = 6.5

Directions: Write the name for each figure.

line AB   ray A   segment CD   angle EFG

Directions: Find the perimeter of each object.

16 ft.   10 ft.   18 ft.

103

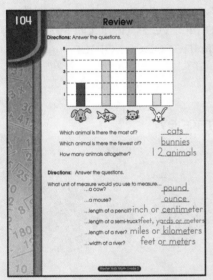

104

Review

Directions: Answer the questions.

Which animal is there the most of? — cats
Which animal is there the fewest of? — bunnies
How many animals altogether? — 12 animals

Directions: Answer the questions.

What unit of measure would you use to measure...
...a cow? — pound
...a mouse? — ounce
...length of a pencil? inch or centimeter
...length of a semi-truck? feet, yards or meters
...length of a river? miles or kilometers
...width of a river? feet or meters

104

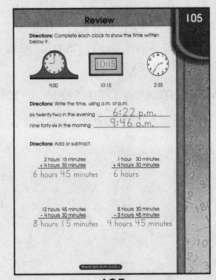

105

Review

Directions: Complete each clock to show the time written below it.

9:00   10:15   2:35

Directions: Write the time, using a.m. or p.m.

six twenty-two in the evening — 6:22 p.m.
nine forty-six in the morning — 9:46 a.m.

Directions: Add or subtract.

$$\begin{array}{c}2\text{ hours }15\text{ minutes}\\+\ 4\text{ hours }30\text{ minutes}\\\hline 6\text{ hours }45\text{ minutes}\end{array} \qquad \begin{array}{c}1\text{ hour }30\text{ minutes}\\+\ 4\text{ hours }30\text{ minutes}\\\hline 6\text{ hours}\end{array}$$

$$\begin{array}{c}12\text{ hours }45\text{ minutes}\\-\ 4\text{ hours }30\text{ minutes}\\\hline 8\text{ hours }15\text{ minutes}\end{array} \qquad \begin{array}{c}8\text{ hours }30\text{ minutes}\\-\ 3\text{ hours }45\text{ minutes}\\\hline 4\text{ hours }45\text{ minutes}\end{array}$$

105

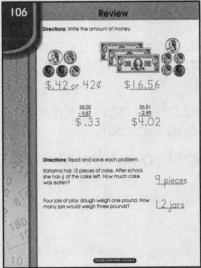

106

Review

Directions: Write the amount of money.

$.42 or 42¢ $16.56

$$\begin{array}{c}\$5.00\\-\ 4.67\\\hline \$.33\end{array} \qquad \begin{array}{c}\$6.51\\-\ 2.49\\\hline \$4.02\end{array}$$

Directions: Read and solve each problem.

Katarina has 12 pieces of cake. After school, she has $\frac{1}{4}$ of the cake left. How much cake was eaten? — 9 pieces

Four jars of play dough weigh one pound. How many jars would weigh three pounds? — 12 jars

106

Money

Talk with your child about different things he or she can do to earn money.

Pose this question to your child: If we did not have money, what would we use to buy things? Tell your child about the Native American system of using wampum as money. Do research together about other monetary systems.

Make money dominoes together.

Let your child practice coins with amounts of money.

Time

Talk with your child about different methods of keeping time, such as clocks, stopwatches, calendars, etc. Let your child make a list of as many ways to keep time as he or she can.

Have your child time how long it takes the family to eat dinner. Have him or her write down the start time, the stop time, and subtract.

Have your child make a time management chart to plan his or her time from after school until bedtime.

Addition, Subtraction, Multiplication, Division

Have your child compute his or her age in years, in months, and in days. Then, try your age!

Purchase a blank book or notebook to serve as your child's Math Journal. As you complete pages in *Master Skills Math* together, your child can write his or her reflections about what he or she has learned. If your child wants, you can write comments to him or her in the book to give your child positive feedback and reinforce the skill learned.

Talk with your child about how math is used in your profession. Make a list of other occupations, and talk about how math is used in these professions as well.

Imagine that "National Math Day" has become a holiday. Ask your child: If you were in charge of the celebration, what math events would you plan?

Measurement

Discuss with your child instruments, other than rulers, that are used to measure (thermometer, calendar, clock, etc.).

Let your child make predictions about the length and weight of various object around your house. Then, have him or her measure the objects to find their actual length or weight. For an extension of this activity, try measuring the same objects with metric measuring tools.

Graphing

Graph the birthdays in your family by the months in which family members were born. Then, ask your child questions to help him or her interpret the graph: In which month(s) do most family members have birthdays? In which month(s) are there the fewest number of birthdays? etc.

Graph the favorite foods of family members, or record the foods your family has eaten over the course of a week, and graph them by food groups. Have your child suggest other things to graph.

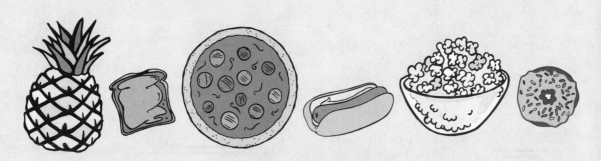